Find Your
BALANCE
In an
Out of Balance
WORLD

Barbara Tessari

Book Design: Gaea L. Honeycut

Dedication

I lovingly dedicate this book to my mother, father,
and brother, Jeff,
who are no longer with us
but will always be in my heart.

Disclaimer

The information contained in this book is based on sound scientific nutrition principles and generally practiced psychology. However, as with any diet and exercise education, the content of this book is only a guideline and considers the author's opinion. Consult your personal health care provider before starting any dietary or exercise program.

Preface

*I*n 2002, I wrote a book entitled *The Pizza and Ice Cream Diet* because I had something to say. I had spent 30 years struggling with food, my unhealthy lifestyle and my obsession with the mirror and the scale. The book was an autobiography of sorts of the experiences, observations and conclusions of being a life-long dieter. The book also gave readers a new direction to find their path to overcoming unhealthy behaviors and to liberate themselves from the struggles I had. You see, after 30 years, I became a person I thought I could never be. I found moderation and balance. I learned to eat when I was hungry, stop eating when I was full, and to move my body just because it felt better. I learned to enjoy all food and treat food equally. I became able to listen to my body when making lifestyle choices instead of what someone told me I was supposed to do. This was an amazing transformation that didn't have to be measured by the mirror or the scale. So, I wanted to tell the world what I discovered about myself to help others do the same. My readers, who could relate to my story, understood the message, applied it and made big changes in their lives.

My personal struggles are now a thing of the past and I have spent the last six years focusing on others and, particularly, observing society. We are living in a very crazy world. Obesity, stress and lack of exercise is a huge problem – and it is affecting nearly everyone. It is very difficult to escape the unhealthy environment we live in and the situation is ruining people's quality of life and causing economic consequences. Most people who ordinarily would not have had a weight problem are now borderline obese, and people who would have had a weight problem are now morbidly obese.

My reason for writing this book is because I have something else to say. It's like I want to scream out a window, "Wake up, people! Don't you see what's going on here? Save yourselves!"

So how do you save yourself? The same way I saved myself. Unlike *The Pizza and Ice Cream Diet*, this book doesn't just speak to readers who are overweight because of food issues, but those who are also just caught up in the unhealthy environment our society has created. You wake up one morning, look in the mirror 20 pounds heavier and say, "What happened to me?"

My hope is that many people will change their lives by taking a few hours to read what I have to say. Maybe I won't provide a way to magically transform yourself, but if I can just get you to think "hmm... I never thought of it that way," maybe you will take a few small steps towards change or at least your readiness for change. You may want to reread the book when the message starts to fade away as you go about your busy life. One thing for sure is, if you are going to invest time and energy to learn how to get healthier and be happier, the time you invest in this book will not be wasted.

I wish you a happy, healthy life!

Table of Contents

1

Can We Find Balance in an Out of Balance World?

*O*ver the last 20 or so years, our environment and the way we live have dramatically changed. Our nation's obsession with food and our resistance to moving our body, along with our hectic work and social standards, have overtaken our lives. We live in an extremely unbalanced, toxic environment and it is degrading our health and the quality of our lives.

The Centers for Disease Control reports that the top three causes of death are smoking, obesity and alcohol – all three are directly related to lifestyle behaviors. Statistics say, two-thirds of Americans are overweight or obese, 80 percent do not get the minimum recommended five fruits and vegetables a day, only 23 percent get regular, daily physical activity, and many of us are living in a state of chronic stress. We are living longer, but sicker, at a huge cost to our country. Obesity-related medical expenses contribute to the highest medical costs and the surgeon general calls obesity a "preventable epidemic," warning that if we don't do something to turn things around, we could be headed for an economic crisis. With all the science, knowledge and resources we have available to us, how could this have happened?

ENVIRONMENT AND SOCIAL EVOLUTION

It seems the origin of the epidemic stems mostly from our environmental and social evolution. Why wasn't obesity an epidemic years ago? Because we lived, thought and behaved differently back then. Food had its place and we had simple, almost unspoken rules about excesses and what we needed in order to enjoy good health – all based more on common sense rather than science. For the most part, we simply listened to our body's natural wants and needs and we didn't follow a theory, method or plan.

In the earliest of times, we spent our days just trying to stay alive. We didn't use our brain much; we used our bodies. We responded to our natural reaction to fear, anger and love, but our biological need for food was essential for survival, and it wasn't readily available. So we spent our days foraging for food or cultivating the fields – all requiring physical energy to accomplish. It was a luxury to be able to consume more calories than we expended at the end of the day.

As we evolved, we began to use our brain more and more – the invention of the wheel, the automobile, the washer and dryer. Then came the TV, the remote control and, during the last 5 to 10 years, BOOM – technology took over and our world changed dramatically. Today, with computers, cell phones, IM, texting and Crackberries (the nickname used for our addictive Blackberries), we are using our brains – some of us nearly 24/7 – and our bodies are sitting idly by. Our brains are getting burned out from overexertion. Our bodies are breaking down from lack of maintenance and are in need of repair.

That's not to say that people weren't overweight years ago. Heck, I was one of them. But, you rarely saw someone who was really obese – the size we see walking down the street today outside of the sideshow at a circus. To be obese, you had to work at it – have "issues" with food. Today, you can fall victim to obesity without even knowing it. Food is everywhere, served in large quantities and you don't even have to get out of your car to have it. Somewhere down the line, we lost respect for food, its purpose and our responsibility to take care of ourselves, and we are relying on high cost medical care to fix the outcome.

It's not like we deliberately became irresponsible and defiant. Rather, the situation just evolved without us being aware of it. For example, years ago, in order to eat the amount of calories and nutrition in a typical coffee house muffin of today, you would have to eat the equivalent of 12 Oreos. We all knew eating 12 Oreos was excessive and unacceptable, so for the most part, we didn't do it – especially first thing in the morning. But a softball-sized muffin is served at nearly every business meeting continental breakfast, so why wouldn't it be perfectly acceptable to also down one at the red light as you are rushing off to work – along with your 300-calorie Starbucks "cup of Joe?" When McDonalds began in 1965 they sold children's Happy Meals as an adult dinner – about 600 calories. Today, the typical adult meal is twice that amount. When growing up, a trip to a restaurant – even a fast food restaurant – was a special treat and not a whim decided on our way from Target to Costco.

OZZIE AND HARRIET WE AREN'T

Our environment has changed and it does bring challenges. When we were growing up, most of our food was prepared in the home. Mom knew what was good for us and set the nutritional standards we followed. Often today, Mom isn't home to shop for and prepare dinner, and no one is looking out for our best interests when it comes to our nutritional needs and to help keep us in line. Many of us don't even have dinner time. We simply eat whenever some kind of food is available to us. "Are you hungry?" and "Do you want something to eat?" are two different questions.

Mom would encourage us to eat, but what she was pushing was something like roast beef, braised potatoes and carrots, and you had to eat these foods before you had dessert (i.e., fat and sugar) – a treat. Breakfast was at home, lunch came in a brown bag, we weren't allowed to pick at food or we would "spoil our dinner," and eating out at a restaurant was savored for special occasions. Even though Mom cooked with butter and lard, most foods were not served with a layer of cheese on top in portions that equal nearly a day's worth of fat and calories. While we had processed food, the amount and quantity was in balance with "real" food, and the appalling amounts of excesses we have today would have been considered gluttonous, wasteful and definitely not condoned.

Physical activity was part of our everyday life and we weren't resistant to it. Today, we "exercise" and most of us fall into two categories:

the active and the inactive. The active invest in special equipment and clothing, go to gyms, run marathons and join expensive clubs just to play tennis. Meanwhile, the majority of Americans' activity consists of walking from point A to point B, and the distance keeps getting shorter and shorter. For these Americans, exercise has become a dirty word and is avoided as much as possible.

Children's recreation used to be right outside the door – kickball in the street, hopscotch, riding bikes – and you weren't allowed in the house until dinner. That was the rule. Today, our children are either overloaded with several structured community sport leagues at one time, or sitting on the couch 12 hours a day playing video games. And if, by chance, a child decides to try out for a sport for the first time at age nine, they are rejected or designated to sit on the bench because they didn't start playing at age four. There just don't seem to be many outlets for simple play any more.

Today, everyone is overbooked, including our children, and that is the social norm. If you aren't stressed out, then you must not have enough to do. There is good stress and bad stress. Most of us are teetering on distress and we are proud of it and like to complain about it. Our minds are in a constant state of stimulation – going, going and, for some of us, not going anywhere except downhill.

To top it off, as our waistlines get larger, the industry has decided to make the criteria smaller. If your BMI is 25 you are healthy. If it's 26 . . . well, you better lose a pound or two so you can satisfy the guidelines, because now you are unhealthy.

I could go on and on citing these scenarios and realities of today's world, and I'm sure you've heard most of it before. The point is we have created a fertile ground for the epidemic to spread, and we must do something about it before it obliterates our economy and our health.

COMPOUNDING THE PROBLEM

With the growing problem, research and science have spent billions of dollars trying to find a solution to the epidemic and they have done nothing to solve the problem. In fact, they've made the situation worse. Instead of helping people adapt to today's environment with common sense and awareness, we have been trying to find a new and better way to tackle the problem. This has just complicated things and has only made it harder to maneuver our way around our toxic environment.

Instead of just eating less and moving more, we have labeled nearly every food as good or bad, healthy or unhealthy. And we have made exercise something that is timed, structured and only effective if we are using the right equipment.

> *You're eating a potato? Well, blah-blah says they are high in sugar and are bad for you. But wait, blah-blah says that potatoes are good for you. This cereal box says it has whole grain. That must be good for me so I'll eat that. But, then, isn't that a processed food? I've heard that's not good. Here is a list of the seven super foods, eat all of these and you will be healthy. But don't eat wheat or drink milk, because that is what is causing cancer. This study says that wine is bad for you; this study says it's good for you. Wait, here's another article that says... Is it better to use a treadmill or an elliptical. Which one will get me in shape the fastest? I just joined this awesome gym with state-of-the-art equipment and I'm going to go four times a week.*

You haven't even regularly taken a 10-minute walk in the last six months! We are spending money trying to achieve ultimate fitness when we haven't even gotten in the habit of regularly putting on our sneakers.

We are on information overload. Many of the solutions to our problems are nothing short of slick marketing campaigns that, when stripped of their believability factors, are nothing more than the snake oil wagons that moved from town to town in the Old West. Studies are confusing and typically isolate only one factor in an overall diet, and the results keep changing depending on the company backing the study.

Our solutions have only made our country more fat and unhealthy than ever, and it seems the more we try to fix the problem the more broken it gets. We have made the ideal lifestyle too hard to achieve, and we have made what used to be simple and natural to us complicated and confusing. Being healthy has become just one more thing to add to our overwhelming list of things to do. It's just too hard to do the "health" thing and we don't want to think about it.

IGNORANCE IS BLISS

Thirty years ago we knew very little about the value of food. There wasn't much science, research or theory behind the issue yet, most of us didn't have a problem. We didn't really talk about it. Back then, we rarely used the term "exercise" or dissected the food pyramid – we didn't have the food pyramid. Very few people ran marathons, joined gyms or downed protein shakes and supplements, and they weren't revered for doing it. A good figure meant a shapely pair of legs and beauty came in many sizes. We naturally made pretty good decisions for the most part . We didn't really need a guidebook to show us how. We just reacted to our body's natural instincts. "Everything in moderation" was the simple mantra for making the right decision.

We ate when we were hungry and stopped eating when we were full. When we felt a little sluggish, we took a walk. We ate breakfast, lunch and dinner, and dessert was always acceptable. If our belts became a little tight, we would forego dessert or not take a second helping for a few weeks because buying a bigger size was a big deal. With today's comfort clothes it's easy to slip into bigger sizes. And we seem to clothes-shop every week, so it's easy to creep up in size without ever acknowledging it. To help us out, clothing marketers acknowledge this and have let the seam out of the perfect size eight to accommodate our denial.

As a result of the over-analysis of what we should eat and how we should move, we have ignored our biological instincts in favor of a process, theory or diet. The result is a dysfunctional relationship with food and a resistance to moving our bodies.

So, with all of the information overload, have we really learned anything worthwhile?

WHOSE FAULT IS IT?

Before this epidemic, an unhealthy lifestyle was viewed as one's choice in a free country – a personal decision. We were responsible for our own behaviors. But here's the problem: our environment is sabotaging us, and sometimes we don't even know the impact our personal decisions have on us. Our society is designed for unhealthy behaviors and it's hard to escape it. We all try to fit in, assimilate and follow the course. Today, we have to make a constant, conscious effort not to fall victim to it. We don't have to be secret eaters or have issues with food. We are bombarded by food that is void of nutrition and extremely high in calories. And we eat it because, sometimes, it's almost expected of us and, sometimes it's the only thing that is available to us. We don't recognize how much food or what types of food our bodies need. Instead, we are responding to our environment or listening to the latest sound bite of the day.

As a society, we conform to social norms. The problem is, our society's normal has become abnormal. It is not uncommon to be munching on a bag of carrots at your desk and have someone walk by and say, "Oh, look at you! Aren't you being good today?" because eating a vegetable is now something out of the ordinary.

It is not normal to eat a 500-calorie muffin for breakfast. It's not normal to have a 1500-calorie meal consisting of two days' worth of sodium and fat and no vegetables. It's not normal to eliminate carbohydrates or fat from your diet. And, it's not normal to be sitting on your butt 16 hours a day.

If our social norms are consuming 3000 calories a day, offering every convenience available so we don't have to move, and creating an environment where stress is expected and workaholics are revered, then that's what most of us will follow just to fit in.

CAN WE DO ANYTHING ABOUT IT?

Our environment sets the stage for unhealthy behaviors, but we don't have to fall in line like zombies. If someone told you to jump off a cliff, would you? Food will always be there. It's up to us to make the decision not to eat it. The couch is always an option. It's up to us to get off of it. So, we have to stop using our environment as an excuse not to change and to act as if it is not in our control. It is totally in our control.

This is America, where freedom rings and the free market rules. The reality is, if we didn't buy it, marketers wouldn't sell it. If we didn't believe it, they wouldn't try to bamboozle us. Changing our dysfunctional environment lies within each one of us. The country will change when we start fighting back instead of giving in to it. The question is, are you going to fight it or succumb to it? If you shift your thinking that the environment is wrong and you want to support its change, you are off to a good start.

PERSONAL RESPONSIBILITY

We have a national health care crisis and everyone is looking to the government to do something about it. We are looking in the wrong direction for help with our problem. The key to managing costs is personal responsibility. It's each and every one of us who uses the health care system. And right now, most of us abuse it. Until we can reduce the NEED for care, the problem is going to escalate. And that involves all of us taking some personal responsibility for our health. The Centers for Disease Control report that 50-75 percent of health care costs are due to unhealthy lifestyle behaviors. With advances in medical technology we are able to live longer lives, but because we don't take care of ourselves, the quality of our lives is terrible and our extended mortality is a huge expense to our country. If our society could just stop the excesses that are causing unnecessary illness, we most likely would have plenty of health care dollars to pay for every man, woman and child who needs care.

THE TIMES THEY ARE A-CHANGING

The good news is that there has been a shift in the environment for the better. We are finally seeing signs that the diet revolution is dying off and common sense is re-emerging. While this is still a free country and we can eat, smoke and drink ourselves to death, the powers that be have been pushing – not to tell us what to do, but to help guide us away from the evils of our environment. For example:

◆ New York City has recently required that all fast food and chain restaurants list the nutritional value of the foods they serve, allowing customers to make educated choices. You can still eat whatever artery-clogging, waistline-busting entrée you want, but at least you will know it is what it is. Education and awareness are the best steps to change. California has fallen in line with similar requirements.

◆ Now that people are realizing their morning visit to Starbucks for their 400 calorie latte has resulted in another 10 pounds, struggling Starbucks is offering healthier breakfast choices of more calorie controlled protein and whole grain foods.

◆ After years of avoidance, the calorie is back. The calorie is the only proven science behind weight gain or loss. We've spent years trying to find a better way to lose weight – only there isn't any.

◆ Employers are starting to recognize that if they want their employees to be healthier, maybe they ought to look around and see if the work environment isn't a big part of the problem.

◆ The BMI (Body Mass Index), which was supposed to be a better indicator of one's health, is being debunked. Apparently, under this measurement system, nearly everyone is overweight – even George Clooney. What is being revealed now is that it's not so much our BMI, but what foods we eat and how physically active we are. We don't have to be thin to be healthy. What a relief to those genetically challenged individuals who have been feeling ashamed of themselves when they truly have been doing the right things. And it helps make the goal easier to achieve and give hope to the average person.

♦ Gyms are becoming more like family recreational centers, where the fit and the fat can play together without discrimination.

These trends are setting the stage to transform our social norms, which will make it easier for all of us to personally implement change. By supporting these positive lifestyle trends, we could slowly achieve a more balanced world.

GOING BACKWARDS TO MOVE FORWARD

Now is the time to take advantage of these changes in the hope of creating an environment around us that is not so unbalanced. We all need to participate to achieve this common goal. But as you know, it's not that simple. The challenge is how do we, as individuals, undo all the damage that has infested our minds and our bodies due to the environment and the "rules" of the last 20 years?

It seems logical that if our present day environment has contributed to this epidemic, and all the diets, theories and studies have done nothing to help the situation, then a solution might be to go back to the way we used to eat, live and behave. Adapt those basic moderation and balance principles to the environment we must live in today.

WHAT ABOUT YOU?

Can you relate to these changes in your environment? Do you feel that your life is out of balance and that taking care of yourself seems to be just one more thing on your overwhelming list of things to do? Are you stressed out, overweight, out of shape, and just aren't enjoying life? Do you feel guilty for giving in to all the temptations that surround you, confused over what you are supposed to do about it, and feel like the obstacles are just too great for you to overcome? Do you look in the mirror in the morning, unhappy with what you see, and think, "What happened to me?" You are not alone.

I'd like to give you hope that you can find your lifestyle balance in this out of balance world. But the answer doesn't lie in a new diet, process, theory or pill. The answer lies within you.

2

What to Expect

*E*ven though we want to change (some of us badly wanting to change), we just can't seem to get away from the problem. We do not have moderation in this world, and we certainly don't have balance. We view our ability to change as an overwhelming task that we just can't handle right now in our busy lives.

So, let's talk about the message I want to deliver to my readers – what to expect from this book. My passion to be a lifestyle coach came from my own experiences, obstacles and success in my personal lifestyle change journey. What I discovered is that it wasn't just about what I was eating, but why and how I was eating it. It wasn't about having the right exercise plan, but getting myself to do it. And it was a lot about changing the reasoning behind why I wanted to change in the first place.

What I ultimately discovered in my own journey was that by shifting the reason behind why I wanted to change, I was better able to change it. The result was not only overcoming my food issues or becoming physically active, but also a continuous quest to have the best quality of life because it was just a better, more enjoyable way to live. That motivation eventually spilled over into making decisions in my life that first bettered me, and then benefited those around me.

WE HAVE MADE IT HARDER THAN IT HAS TO BE

Another discovery I made along the way is this: Not only has the American lifestyle made it harder for us to stay balanced, but the diets I had been following were only making it harder than it had to be. For most of us, the outward signs of our unhealthy lifestyle and poor quality of life are weight gain and, possibly, obesity. It's what we visually see as a result of our unhealthy behaviors. It sort of labels us, and so we do anything to get rid of that label – we are on a quest to get thin without recognizing that it's not about erasing the external outcome through diet and exercise, but figuring out how you got that way in the first place. To focus on what it is doing to your quality of life, not the mirror and the scale. That said, much of the problem does lie in what and how much we are eating, so weight maintenance is a big part of achieving a balanced lifestyle and will be discussed primarily in this book. I hope to eventually enable you to understand the subtle but major difference between just losing weight and achieving a balanced lifestyle.

Regarding the challenge of helping people get over their negative lifestyle behaviors, a close friend who is also a nutritionist told me that most of us don't realize "It's not really that hard to lose weight and live a healthier lifestyle. It's just easier not to; so we don't."

There is a lot of truth in this statement. The simple actions one takes to improve negative lifestyle behaviors are: to include better nutrition in your daily diet, eat a bit less, move a little more and do these things consistently. That simple program has become an overwhelming obstacle for us, due in large part to our inundation by hundreds of theories of other ways to do it and faster ways to achieve it.

So, the last thing I want to do is provide you with another way to do it or make promises to you that don't deliver. I don't propose a new theory or process to help you lose weight, or offer a magic secret to physical fitness or eliminating stress. To the contrary, we're going to go back to the old way, which was easier to follow and seemed to work just fine throughout time. After all, this obesity epidemic is new. We lived for thousands of years without this daunting problem.

I figured out that the old way was the easy way by accident. As I adapted my own solutions to my negative lifestyle behaviors, instigated by my newfound goal of simply achieving a better quality of life, I discovered my new "way" was actually nothing new, but very familiar to me. I had naturally adapted to simple moderation and balance principles. I soon found myself reciting, not the latest sound bite from MSN, but the old sayings of yesteryear – like, "I think I'll go take a walk and work up an appetite." I never really knew the meaning of this old fashioned statement our grandmothers would say, until I naturally experienced it.

The goal of this book is not for the reader to be the healthiest person on the planet. It's about achieving a more balanced lifestyle that takes into consideration your likes, dislikes, environment, weaknesses and strengths. You will discover "your" way to achieving success in your journey from an unhealthy lifestyle that is dragging you down, to a balanced lifestyle that can liberate you and provide a better quality of life. *Find Your Balance* offers you the flexibility to do this without giving up anything in the process. A way that, when implemented, you can look back and say, "Gee, that was a lot easier than I thought!" And most importantly, a way that helps you accomplish a change you can maintain and enjoy for the rest of your life.

THE PATH YOU'LL TAKE

When writing a self-help book, an author is advised to offer a "whatever" step plan or specific process – an easy-to-follow program that the reader can adopt and then be "cured" of whatever issue for which he needs help. I struggled with this because, as I see it, changing your lifestyle is more of a journey, with different roads for different people. A journey full of wrong turns and dead ends and, eventually, if you stick with it, you'll find your way. Changing your lifestyle, or not changing, isn't a straight path with simple directions. What I'll try to do is provide a map with many paths to choose.

So, this book is not intended to be a technical explanation of achieving good health filled with charts and graphs and statistics. Nor is it a book that explores all of your emotional baggage that haunts you and keeps you from change. Nor is it a specific step-by-step process that will transform you. If I were to provide you with all the possible detailed information on how to live a healthy lifestyle or what is at the root of your problem, this would be a very thick book that would probably end up stuffed in a drawer or retired on a shelf along with all the other diet books you've attempted to read.

We are all short on time, so I wanted you to be able to read this in a few hours, get a new perspective on what's going on with *you*, explore some simple thoughts and ideas on what you can do to change it, and contemplate and be motivated to do something about it. Once you know your obstacles, you can take action to overcome them. Most of the time, the answer is not complicated and you'll find it's your answer, not someone else's. If you asked a hundred people who changed their lifestyle forever how they did it, you will get many different answers. They may have gotten inspiration or guidance from different sources, but ultimately, the answer was theirs to find.

EXPLORING YOUR ANSWER

While adopting better eating habits and increasing physical activity can help you achieve a more balanced and better quality of life, it only applies to the doing part. The bigger obstacle still remains – what is keeping you from change and what is sabotaging your good intentions? For many of us, this is the key to unlocking our answer to looking and feeling our best.

My role as a lifestyle coach is to help individuals find their own answer to the obstacles that keep them from changing their negative lifestyle behaviors. I don't give them the answers. I just guide them in the right direction. In the chapters ahead, you will have the opportunity to explore all the reasons why you may not have been successful at changing your behaviors in the past, and why you have been so caught up in the toxicities of today's environment. You will have the opportunity to become your own lifestyle coach – prepare yourself for change, ask yourself questions, contemplate your actions, and learn how to stop dieting and start living healthfully because it is who you are, not what you are pretending to be. The goal is not to race to the finish line but to make changes that you can enjoy forever.

In addition to the actionable solutions, you need to also address mental obstacles that keep you from change. Identifying your mental obstacles will help you find simple ways to overcome them. We'll talk about a lot of different reasons why we don't make good decisions – bad habits, blinders, taste adaptation, denial, stress, addiction to diets. For most of us, it isn't just one reason but a combination of negative behaviors that result in weight gain, ill health and imbalance. Some will apply to you; others may not. Our environment is a contributing factor to these reasons and is causing the problem to grow. Adapting healthier behaviors in spite of our toxic world and in spite of our negative thoughts can be a challenge, but by changing your thinking you can overcome them. This book can help you contemplate what thoughts, actions and behaviors keep you from making good decisions.

Most of all, *Find Your Balance* will change your perspective on why you are setting out to make changes in the first place, and give you the motivation and ease to do it. The ultimate conclusion to discovering and applying your answer is that you become truly liberated. You don't have to think about it any more. You've actually solved the problem. Gone. Move on to something else.

My hope is that you will take the time to read this book and do a little self-exploration so you can point yourself in the right direction for lifelong change. To first take a step back and identify the problems that have been really keeping you from change, and then set out to take action to change them. No promises, no guaranteed results, no magic solution. But maybe, in the process you might find the magic in you to achieving your balance in an out of balance world.

Finding Your Balanced Lifestyle

Find Your Balance is about discovering your own path to a balanced lifestyle. The best way to explain a "balanced" lifestyle is to observe people who don't seem to be affected by the negative environment we live in, or caught up in the diet and food frenzy. I'm not talking about the types who are: all-natural, organic, yoga, marathon runners, don't eat sugar or wheat or dairy, or who are vegetarian (not that there is anything wrong with those types). I'm talking about the people who don't talk about their weight or their exercise program or analyze their imperfect bodies. They aren't overweight and they seem to be pretty healthy and happy.

If you ask them, "How do you do it?" they'll typically answer "Do what?" and then will say things like, "I eat everything in moderation. I eat when I'm hungry; I stop when I'm full. I walk my dog. I love chocolate and eat it every day. I weigh myself once a year at the doctor's office. I stop and smell the flowers." For the most part, a person like this has a normal reaction to food and a balanced life.

She lives by the principles of moderation and balance – just like we did years ago. And, just as in my case, the rules that may stir in the back of her head are more the ones that came from her grandmother and not what the latest diet guru or the news is reporting today.

HEALTHY VERSUS BALANCED

I choose to use the term balanced lifestyle rather than healthy lifestyle because the latter term has been so overused, and it has a negative connotation with many who are frustrated because they can't live up to the ideal. The actual definition of healthy living is "the steps, actions and strategies one puts in place to achieve optimum health." That definition sounds pretty intense and difficult to achieve – especially if you currently enjoy your beer and chicken wings, or chocolate and butter. For many of us, a healthy lifestyle assumes that everything we do fits into a category of healthy or unhealthy and this makes it very hard for us to achieve, so we get frustrated and give up. When you read the hundreds of diets that may categorize foods like meat, dairy, wheat, apples, bananas, potatoes and such as being unhealthy, your food options get pretty limited and illogical.

A balanced lifestyle follows the principles of moderation and balance. It looks at your lifestyle as a whole but is liberally holistic. It's not about the Big Mac that you ate, but how you balanced it out with other actions over a period of time. It's not about the time on the treadmill, but responding to the activity your body craved. It's not about avoiding stress, but taking steps to balance stress with relaxation so you can have a fulfilling life that doesn't get out of control. It allows you to enjoy everything in moderation, which satisfies your body's wants and needs for good health, while giving you the freedom to indulge reasonably. If you can see everything balanced, then you open up the possibility that decisions can be made by simply asking your body what it wants and trusting, that it will tell you the right thing. To me, life without the sip of a fine wine or a really good piece of chocolate would negatively impact the joy in my life. But, at the same time, I need to be responsible about it or else I will pay the price.

MODERATION AND BALANCE

Moderation and balance is as simple as it sounds. Eat a balance of all foods and eat them in moderation – meaning, not too many calories. Move your body freely because it wants to move, without getting caught up in a process or achieving a specific goal. Stay away from excesses in life and be aware of how your body reacts to them. The goal is to make a decision simply because you feel better for it. And that, in and of itself, becomes the compelling reason to do it.

The problem is that the diet revolution has thrown moderation and balance to the wayside in favor of our making decisions based on a book, theory or process, and our unbalanced environment has made it easier to make not-so-good decisions. Today we have learned to make decisions with our minds and our eyes. With dieting mindsets, we forbid ourselves certain foods or feel guilty eating them, and the result is confusion and resistance. Our environment allows us to fall in line with what is going on with everyone else without thinking for ourselves. We see everyone else eat a donut, so we do too, without asking ourselves if we are even hungry or craving something sweet. Not that a donut is bad for you. After all, God gave us a sweet tooth. We should satisfy it. But there is a time and place for everything, and your body most likely doesn't want a sugar rush for breakfast.

With moderation and balance thinking, you simply have to listen to yourself. If you haven't moved your body, your body wants to move. If you aren't hungry, don't eat and when you've eaten enough, stop. Your body naturally craves a balance of all foods and it doesn't like it when it's not satisfied, and it doesn't like it when it's stuffed. If you are feeling lethargic and your joints ache, then it's time to get up and move around. If stress is causing you headaches, sleepless nights and irritability, then it's time to listen to your body, take more control of the situation, and do something about it. When you don't listen to your body, your actions negatively impact your joy and you don't feel at your best – you are out of balance.

GRANDMA'S RULES

Moderation and balance was a simple way we lived years ago and it worked. We didn't have Dr. Phil, Atkins, Bob Greene. Oprah's newest friend Dr. Oz and the hundreds of other diet "gurus." We had Mom or Grandma. Grandma had a few rules to follow to make sure her loved ones were healthy. You ate what she told you to because she knew best. She prepared and served your food – not Applebee's or

Nutri-System – and your Mom would simply slap your hand when you picked at dinner before she put it on the table. There was a book of etiquette we followed because that's what was expected of society – no questions asked.

While these rules weren't very scientific, the message was pretty much the same – only without millions of dollars of research, studies, analysis and contradictions – and it didn't require a 300-page book to figure it out. They were easy to understand guidelines that encompassed most everything needed to live a balanced lifestyle.

Eat three square meals a day

Eat a balance of all foods spread throughout the day – breakfast, lunch and dinner. If you are hungry, have a snack – maybe even a cookie (the size of a jelly jar lid, not the size of a Frisbee).

You can't have dessert until you finish your supper

Supper was typically meat and vegetables; dessert was fat and sugar. Today, dinner is mostly fat and sugar and then we eat dessert on top of it.

Eat your vegetables; an apple a day keeps the doctor away

There didn't have to be a lot of science behind it, but Grandma knew that vegetables and fruit had vitamins and minerals the body needed to keep the doctor away. So, we ate them because she said so, and Grandma knew best.

Don't leave the house without breakfast

If you didn't eat breakfast, then you weren't having your three square meals. It doesn't take a scientist to know that if you haven't eaten in 12 hours, then you probably should eat something before you go off to school or work. Ironically, most people who do not eat breakfast are overweight.

If you eat too much you'll have a bellyache

It is not wise to eat so much that you are uncomfortable. Today, many of us don't eat until we are full – we eat until we are stuffed – and that means we overeat, resulting in being overweight.

Don't talk with your mouth full

We had table manners and etiquette rules we followed, which have become a lost art today. We gobble down food that results in eating too many calories and not paying attention to our food. And, yes, many of us talk with our mouths full!

Don't spoil your dinner

It wasn't common practice to eat between meals. We weren't allowed to hang out in the kitchen, stop at a fast food joint on a whim while shopping, or get something to eat unless it was the proper time. Otherwise, we wouldn't be hungry for the healthy meal that Mom worked so hard preparing.

Go out and play!

When we were kids we weren't allowed to sit around the house. I can remember having to go outside to play in the rain, armed with an umbrella and galoshes.

Go work up an appetite

If you did spoil your dinner, you could go out and play to burn off some calories to stimulate your appetite.

Get to bed!

Sleep was important and most of us got enough of it because our lives weren't in such chaos. Today, a good night's rest is considered a luxury and is practiced by few.

These familiar sayings provided you with most of the rules to follow to maintain a healthy quality of life. We will apply Grandma's rules to today's world as we take our journey to a balanced life.

DISCOVERING YOUR OBSTACLES TO LIFESTYLE BALANCE

Find Your Balance applies moderation and balance principles with a few of these simple rules. However, while the concept is simple, it's application is not always easy. We've spent years developing our unhealthy behaviors and our negative mindsets and habits. Without a "de-programming" of your thoughts, actions and behaviors, you will fall into interpreting the intent of this book as just another diet. The process will be confusing and the message may get lost in translation.

While we will talk a lot about how to lose weight, get more physically active and improve your overall health, those aims are not the driving focus. It's more about becoming the type of person I talked about before – someone who simply has a balanced lifestyle. I want to liberate you to become one of "those people" who doesn't have issues with food, their weight or their lifestyle. As I said, the primary goal of a balanced lifestyle is to feel better – to have a better quality of life. Weight loss and better health are simply an added bonus. If you think you are giving up something, or that eating right and getting exercise is a sacrifice, program or process, you will most likely falter. You have to enjoy the changes you make and it becomes a natural way of life.

ACCOUNTABILITY, ACKNOWLEDGEMENT, AWARENESS

Throughout the journey, we are going to point out your unique obstacles that are igniting your unhealthy behaviors and keeping you from change. Most of us focus on what we should or shouldn't do to achieve weight loss or good health – which is important. But, in reality, most of our problem lies with how and why we do it – or don't do it.

The philosophy of this book is centered around three guiding principles to help you with your journey: Accountability, Acknowledgement and Awareness. These principles will help you understand moderation and balance, discover the obstacles that are holding you back, and learn how to listen to your body and not your mind.

Accountability

Be accountable for your actions. Most of us are very stressed with an overload of responsibilities and we become accountable to everyone but ourselves. As a result, many of us continue to fail at overcoming negative lifestyle behaviors, no matter how hard we try, because we put blinders on and don't own up to our actions as a coping mechanism. Blinders come in the form of excuses, denial, justification and blame. We will take the blinders off and help you eliminate the excuses and admit your destructive actions. Being true to yourself will open up the possibility of real lifestyle change.

Acknowledgement

If you can acknowledge your actions before taking them, you can make better decisions. Bad habits can sabotage our intentions: moments of mindless eating, eating too fast, and stress or emotional eating. By simply being aware that these actions are taking place, you can put forth an effort to stop or control them.

Acknowledge the impact on your well-being of the decisions that you make. Shifting your motivation from a specific goal of weight loss or achieving a health status to the immediate ongoing reward of simply feeling better can greatly influence your ability to make better decisions.

Awareness

Be aware of what your body wants and needs. Today, our basic biological need for proper nutrition and physical movement is being ignored and substituted by a process, a reprimand, a theory or a diet.

You will learn how to tap into your body's signals again to influence your decisions. Once this is accomplished you can make better decisions, naturally, liberating yourself from your negative lifestyle behaviors.

Become aware of the things in the surrounding environment that are sabotaging your efforts to make better lifestyle decisions. Our society is full of deceptions, untruths and sales tactics that leave us confused, ill-educated and bound to fail. We will unravel the gobbledygook and re-educate you on the basic tried and true principles of moderation and balance. You will become a better "consumer" of food.

THE JOURNEY

We're going to start your journey with the reprogramming of your negative mindsets and behaviors by using accountability, acknowledgement and awareness. We will first take off the blinders and hold you accountable for your actions, and then identify behaviors that are sabotaging your efforts to change. Once we've gotten this far in the journey, we can move forward with a new sense of awareness and start tapping into your body's natural behavior signals – liberating yourself, at last, from the negative environment we live in.

We will remind you of the principles of weight loss, good health and what it means to have moderation and balance. In your journey you will find the right balance that fits in with your likes, dislikes, your environment and what you want to achieve. With this valuable information you can design your own balanced lifestyle plan. During the journey, you will hopefully start moving away from the negative thoughts, actions and behaviors that are causing your life to be so unbalanced, and be motivated and empowered to change those negative behaviors and start feeling and looking your best.

But first and foremost, we have to get you ready for change.

4

Are You Ready to Feel Better?

*A*fter coaching many people (including myself) on how to lose weight and change their lifestyle, I am convinced that most anyone can change their behaviors, as long as they are ready. It's overcoming the obstacles most of us face that keep us from achieving what we so desperately want – a better quality of life. Even though you may want to change your lifestyle, you have to be ready to take on the challenge. Otherwise you will fail, just as you've most likely failed at previous attempts to change your behaviors.

You may not have thought much about your readiness factor. "Of course, I'm ready to lose weight, get healthy and feel more balanced. Why wouldn't I be?" But how many times have you said that before without success? To make sure you are prepared to take this journey, we're going to spend some time addressing issues you may not have thought about that might impact your ability to be successful.

EXPECTATIONS

The journey to a balanced lifestyle is not about achieving six-pack abs or losing 20 pounds in a month. If that's what you are looking for, then put the book down. You will not find it here. While I hope this book speaks to most everyone, this book has a special appeal if:

♦ Over the years, you have tried, bought and failed every diet book, theory, product and pill.

- You are at a point in life where you are concerned about what the future holds for you if you do not start making changes in your lifestyle.

- Your sense of well being is imbalanced – not eating right, little exercise, not sleeping well and you, overall, feel like crap and feeling helpless to change it.

- Or, you just woke up one day, looked in the mirror and thought, "Where did these 20 pounds come from?"

You can achieve weight loss, a balanced life and better health, but it will take time to get there. We all have different journeys to travel. Some will get there quickly while others may take more time. As I said, the journey we will take is about finding your way to a balanced life without a set deadline or final destination. We will not measure success by the mirror, the scale or a blood panel number. Rather, it will be measured by the newfound empowerment and desire to make good decisions for yourself, and the enjoyment of the quality of your life that positive change brings.

WHAT IS LIFESTYLE CHANGE?

The term "lifestyle change" has become trendy. Dieting is out; lifestyle change is in. Lifestyle change and dieting are fundamentally two different goals, but it can be a difficult process to help individuals understand the subtle, but important difference.

Both involve changing your health, which includes managing your weight and getting more physical activity. The key differentiator is the motive for doing the action. Dieting is more about changing the way you look or changing your health status, but lifestyle change is about changing the way you live. Lifestyle change has a beginning, but no end. You don't stop and start again. You don't get back into it. You live it. Every day. Lifestyle change is a continuous, joyous journey that, when truly realized, is hard to resist.

While many people say they want a lifestyle change they are not truly ready. They may want to be thin, control their cholesterol, or run a 5K, but they don't truly understand what it means to make a lifestyle change and the ultimate reward it provides. The reality is, unless you are ready to make changes for the rest of your life, why bother?

A GOAL WITHOUT END

The primary objective of lifestyle change is an intangible goal – to feel better. Maintaining your weight, eating a balanced diet, getting regular physical exercise all make you feel better but they are the actions you take – what you do – to achieve the goal. You may say, "I want to live a healthier, better quality of life," but your energy and focus may still be on the specific, tangible goals of weight loss, better cholesterol numbers, etc. because they are defined, familiar and measurable. But, as we know, achieving these specific goals is easier said than done. Some studies say 95 percent of us who start a diet program fail. Most of us fail over and over again. We set out on a new diet, exercise program or other "action" and we end up not losing weight, gain it back, or worse, become a destructive yo-yo dieter. We view the actions we take as a means to an end – the finish line.

The goal of feeling better is not something that, once accomplished, ends. It focuses more on the journey, not the destination. It involves self-exploration to understand, want and accept what you need to do to change the way you are currently living your life and how you feel as a result of your actions. While a defined, measurable goal helps one to stay focused in order to achieve a specific outcome, it can cloud the experience of what is happening along the way. You need to be able to appreciate and feel the experience of lifestyle change.

EASIER SAID THAN DONE

Now you may be saying to yourself, "Oh, okay. Now I see. I want to feel better too, so instead of saying I want to lose weight, I'll say, I want to feel better." Saying it and doing it are very different things. To feel better, you may need to make changes in your life that you will be uncomfortable with, afraid of, or feel you won't like. Maybe you want to lose weight and be healthier, but maybe you don't want to actually live like a thinner, healthier person – ah, ha! That's a problem. If you aren't motivated to want to live like someone who respects good nutrition, moves their body freely and eats moderately, then you are not ready for true lifestyle change.

THOUGHTS IN PREPARATION FOR CHANGE

What is driving your motivation and are you willing to make the changes necessary to do it? Preparing for lifestyle change involves a lot of contemplation. But it's an extremely important step to explore before you even start with the "actions" you will take to change your lifestyle. Let's think about the following questions and then you can consider if you are ready to change before you take action.

- Are you willing to take off the blinders that keep you from change?
- Are you motivated for the right reason?
- Do you believe you can change?
- Do you really want to change?
- Are you ready to stop dieting?
- What are you willing to do to change?
- Are you willing to accept setbacks?
- Will you accept the realities of lifestyle change?

DO YOU HAVE BLINDERS?

Our current status of change readiness can be described, metaphorically, as blinders over our eyes. I don't think anyone really wants to be overweight, out of shape and in ill health, but many of us choose not to even try to change our behaviors – no matter how destructive. Some among us keep the blinders completely closed despite being miserable with diabetes, sleep apnea or other lifestyle related diseases. Deep inside, they have a strong yearning for change. Yet they choose to suppress it, hide it and even defy it. "I'm big and beautiful and happy the way I am." Well, it sounds good and we should respect that, but honestly, most who say this are putting up a front. They may have accepted it, but they wish they could change it.

Most of us, at times, may open the blinds, wake up and say, "Today I am going to change!" only to find that by noon we've already faltered and the motivation we had just hours before gets suppressed somewhere in the back of our brain. The blinds close again.

Or, maybe you are able to consistently stick with your efforts, for a while. You may follow a diet, hire a personal trainer, and religiously go to the gym, but eventually motivation wanes, the blinds start to close and you are right back where you started. This is what happens with yo-yo dieters. They are able to change, temporarily, but their emphasis is on will power. They're focusing on the "what" to do and, more than likely, the goal of seeing a lower number on the scale. Usually, that achievement doesn't come fast enough to keep us motivated. We slip, slide and then we start closing the blinds again as we "cheat" on our diet, miss the trainer appointment, or put off going to the gym yet another day. Then we are right back where we started. Sometimes worse as the guilt sets in, the failure overwhelms us and we just give up. We slip back into our comfortable habits and never really experience lasting change. The blinds close again.

For the majority of us, we keep opening and closing the blinds. We think of the shortsighted goals, not recognizing the Holy Grail. When the goal of lifestyle change is achieved, the blinders come off, the Holy Grail is found – the ability and motivation to change your life – forever. On your journey you will have to constantly remind yourself to keep the blinds open or you will not succeed.

ARE YOU MOTIVATED FOR THE RIGHT REASON?

Let's think about how you can change your motivation from short-term goals to a permanent lifestyle change. The goal to lose weight, reduce cholesterol, etc. requires one to make good decisions over a long period of time. Every time you are faced with an action decision – to take a walk or sit on the couch, to choose the grilled chicken over the cheeseburger – something has to drive you to make the better decision in spite of temptation. Too often, as we've all experienced, even seeing weight loss or health stats change doesn't provide enough motivation because the reward is somewhere down the road. Inevitably, there are times when you're tired, busy or distracted and you start to close the blinds again. It's very easy to do because the goal, the reward, isn't immediate.

For example, say you've decided on a goal to take a two-mile walk after work three times a week. You might even anticipate how you are going to take the walk throughout the day. But then, you get home after a hectic day and, rather than taking your walk, you find yourself on the couch or surfing the Net and the task of taking that walk somehow feels overwhelming. So, you start pushing it out of your mind, delaying the task. Then, ultimately, you make an excuse and justify doing it tomorrow – and often, tomorrow never comes.

On the other hand, if you have the goal of a lifestyle change, you receive immediate gratification for making the good decision. With lifestyle change thinking, when making the decision, you may contemplate, "If I walk, I'll end up enjoying it. I will feel good about myself for doing it. I will reduce stress, have more energy, be in a better mood tonight and get more done in the long run. If I don't, I will be less productive, retain stress, feel tired, and I won't feel good about myself." If you truly want to have a better quality of life, you can be motivated to make better decisions simply because you get the reward and achieve the goal immediately. And, the decision you made also leads you towards the tangible goal of weight loss, better stats, etc.

DO YOU REALLY WANT TO FEEL BETTER?

This may sound like a silly question, but you must ask yourself, "Do I really want to feel better to improve the quality of my life?" I know that sounds crazy – "Of course, I do!" Well, maybe not. And not knowing is a huge obstacle. You see, most of us may want to be thin and get healthier, but we don't want to change our current lifestyle. We think living a healthier lifestyle is a sacrifice. We don't want to give up the pig-outs at the restaurant, or the comfort of our couch – we just want to be thin and healthy. This is why we like to buy into the claims of "eat all you want and still lose weight" or "lose weight without exercise!"

What many of us don't understand is eating healthy foods and getting regular exercise are the reward – not the punishment. If you think that you will miss your negative lifestyle habits, not going back to them will always be a struggle. You have to be open to the possibility that you can become a person who naturally chooses to stop eating when satisfied and not stuffed, or craves the urge to take a stress-reducing walk so much that they actually do it.

Change "I Have To" Into "I Want To"

Changing our thinking from "I have to" to "I want to" can help influence your decisions. Wanting to do something is easier than having to do something. You immediately set yourself up for failure if you've already defined it as something you don't want to do. Focus on what you can have, not what you can't have. When your comfort zone starts to keep you from doing the action, focus on the immediate reward. The reward? You end your day with a good night's sleep – your stomach settled, not indigested; your body tired from the movement it craved; and your mind relaxed because you allowed your "self" what it really wanted. You wake up the next morning, raring to go, rejuvenated and ready to take on the demands of the day.

If you don't believe you will like the change, then why would you want to change? Think about it. People who have lost weight and adapted healthier lifestyles don't say they miss the good old days when they could overeat on junk and not have to exercise. The reality is, you just don't know what you are missing.

DO YOU BELIEVE YOU CAN CHANGE?

When we've tried over and over again to change our behaviors unsuccessfully, we can assume we are who we are and incapable of change. Even though we keep trying, in the back of our minds we think: "I won't be successful." "It's too hard." "I'm not an exercise person." "I'm too old, too fat, too out of shape." "Yeah, right." We cannot imagine ourselves behaving any way other than how we currently do. Me? – A healthy, active, well-balanced person? That's someone else. With this kind of self-sabotaging negative thinking, you are not ready to change. Though we may dream of changing who we are, the overweight, inactive, stressed-out person is all we know and we can't imagine ourselves any other way. If you don't believe you can change, you won't.

So, how do you get yourself to believe you can change? You have the ability to live differently than you do now. It can happen. Millions of people have done it. They believed in themselves. Maybe not totally, but just enough to get started. If you can make just a small positive change in your life, and focus on what the change is doing to you personally, not what the scale is saying or the anticipated final goal, you are on the right path. You can see a glimmer of hope that you can actually change, that you might like the changes, and that small accomplishment can help inspire you to do more.

ARE YOU READY TO QUIT DIETING?

Many of us are brainwashed into the dieting mindset. It's easy to say, "stop dieting," but many of us are conditioned to following diets and cannot think for ourselves. Diets have caused most of us to make decisions with our minds and not our bodies. Many of us are addicted to dieting logic – questioning everything we eat, good food-bad food, can have-can't have, binge and deprivation. Even if we haven't been habitual dieters, some of us feel the effects simply by reading all the studies, theories and media attention dieting brings. The term "going on a diet" implies we are doing something short-term we don't want to do. Going "on a diet" means we expect to go "off the diet." If the goal is to finish the diet, failure most likely will be the outcome.

People who have been successful with popular diets like Weight Watchers will commonly lose 20, 30, even 50 pounds or more, only to gain it all back again. Then we hear them say, "I've got to go back to WW." They go through the effort of losing all that weight, but then don't learn anything in the process and view the goal simply as "losing weight." So, they lose the weight – then what? In their new campaigns, WW is trying to encourage their clients to focus more on the lifestyle change aspect, which is great. But changing the dieting mindset of people is easier said than done.

While it's hard to be successful at dieting, it's even harder to keep the weight off. Think of all the celebrities endorsing Jenny Craig and Nutri-System – they lose weight, showing off on *Oprah*, only to end up on the cover of *National Inquirer* 20 pounds heavier than when they started. That's not to say that people who choose these dieting plans always gain the weight back. If they are successful, they have learned something more valuable along the way.

Altering the way we eat and move are part of the change, but not the only priority. Losing weight occurs when you decide to change other aspects of your life. "Diets" produce the thinking that you'd be happy if only you could lose weight. The truer part of losing weight has more to do with the improved way of life, not the thinner image in the mirror. You can't be a thin person unless you live like a thin person.

Did you ever notice a lot of diet commercials' "after" pictures show not only a thinner person, but also an athletic one? They'll show the transformed person hiking up a hill, jogging or enjoying a salad on the tennis court. They'll talk about the energetic life clients lead now that they are thin. It makes one believe that because they are thin, their life is wonderful. But it's the life transformation that is wonderful – the physical change is just a bonus.

You have to be able to live with the change. You have to incorporate eating and activity changes as part of your daily life – a joyous part of your life. Focusing too much on losing weight can actually cause us to gain weight, and the diet mentality is contributing to the obesity problem in this country. For many of us, what happens is that we start thinking about it too much, and end up only wanting food more because we can't have it. We resist exercising because we have to do it. Getting off the dieting mindset is a bigger obstacle than many realize. The mindset is ingrained in us and, even though we may outwardly change the goal to lifestyle change, our brains are conditioned to revert back to the old mindset.

During the journey, from time to time, you may have to ask yourself as a reminder when making decisions, "Is this a negative dieting reaction that is driving my decision?"

WHAT ARE YOU WILLING TO DO TO CHANGE?

During your journey to a lifestyle change, you will have to contemplate – a lot. You have to face your fears, your doubts, and your current actions – come clean, so to speak. The following are some of the issues we will address during the journey and will be elaborated on in upcoming chapters:

Will you devote the time to contemplate your thoughts and actions?

The blinders I spoke of earlier that keep us from change typically fall into the categories of bad habits, excuses, denial and blame. If you are always reaching for an excuse, go into denial, blame someone or justify something, you will never change. If you have bad habits that are sabotaging your good intentions, but you refuse to recognize and do something about them, then you will always be scratching your head wondering why you're not making progress. Sometimes the thoughts and actions are easy to identify. Others are not – especially when you have been reacting this way for a long time. You have to be willing to continually coach yourself throughout this process to catch yourself putting up those blinders.

Are you willing to change your habits, surroundings and routines?

Unhealthy lifestyles spread through unhealthy surroundings. The workplace, social situations, our obligations and day-to-day duties sabotage us, and we feel hopeless to fight all this. You have to be willing to change your surroundings, resist following the course of society's abnormal behaviors, and think differently about what it means to be good to yourself. If being good to yourself is a pig fest at a local restaurant a few times a week and you aren't willing to modify this routine, then you aren't ready for change. If you think exercise is something that could never be enjoyable, then you will always be fighting to get off the couch. There are many other ways to reward yourself and you must be open to trying new surroundings, habits and ways of life. You can't think of the change as a sacrifice. It must be something you want to do – so think of it more as an option, and then decide to choose the better option because you will feel better for it and it will improve the quality of your life.

Are you ready to respect yourself?

Many of us answer to everyone except ourselves – we are selfless. Not being selfless does not make you selfish. Not being selfless allows you to care about your well-being. We live in a very hectic demanding world and it is very easy to put ourselves last on our list of things to do. We feel guilty taking time for ourselves.

Many of us use our selflessness as an excuse for not living a healthier lifestyle. We conclude that we don't have time, or someone or something else needs us more. Often, we allow everything else to get in the way as a means to avoid taking care of ourselves.

You need to be willing to respect the importance of your health and emotional needs. If you take care of yourself, you will be better able to take on the demands of the day, and with your needs met, take better care of others.

Are you prepared for setbacks?

The journey to lifestyle change is not about being perfect, but having the better decisions outweigh the not so good decisions. It took you years to develop unhealthy habits, so don't expect to change them in a month.

Often we fail at changing our lifestyle because we confuse setbacks with failure. If we beat ourselves up by thinking, "I blew it" or "I can't do this," we've failed. Accept setbacks as a part of the change process and take the opportunity to learn from it and grow. Overcoming setbacks is a great turning point to changing behaviors. Learning from setbacks will help you understand how and why you got off track in the first place, and help you to avoid them in the future.

THE REALITIES OF LIFESTYLE CHANGE

Not only must you be ready for change, but you also must accept certain realities about weight loss and good health. Some of them will be disheartening. But if you can accept these realities, then you are most likely ready to move forward on your path to a better life.

You will probably not reach your ultimate goal

Most of us have unrealistic expectations about our ability to achieve a number on a scale or the body of our dreams. The truth is we aren't supposed to have six-pack abs and buns of steel – well, maybe if you are a genetically gifted 20-year-old athlete. But, 98 percent of us weren't built that way, and trying to become a person you weren't meant to be can be a depressing battle. While it's great to "go for it" and achieve your best, you must also be happy with your progress and not get down on yourself and frustrated for trying to reach for something that is unattainable. Do not believe the smoke and mirror images we see in magazines. If you want to feel good about yourself, do a photo shoot in subdued lighting while striking your best pose, and then do some creative editing in Photoshop. You'd be surprised at how great you can look when you aren't standing in front of your bathroom mirror in your old skivvies.

It will probably take a lot longer to lose weight than you had hoped

The diet industry has led us to believe that you can magically lose lots of pounds by simply following their plan. Most of these claims are highly exaggerated, even impossible. You will learn the realistic expectations for weight loss. Think about how long it took you to gain the weight. Now consider: it's a lot easier to eat the cookie, than not eat the cookie. The good news is, since you will not be depriving yourself or giving up anything, you don't have to be rushing to the finish line. If you like the changes you make in your life, then it doesn't matter how long it takes you to get there.

You get out of it what you put into it

Achieving lifelong change does require effort, and how much effort you put into it will impact your results. If you make minimal changes in your life and maintain them, you are achieving some success. If you are overweight, just a loss of 10 pounds can reduce your chances of preventable disease, increase your energy level and make you feel better. More importantly, if the lifestyle changes you make prevent future weight gain; that is another success. However, if you are hoping to achieve a major milestone of significant proportions, you will have to build on your progress to keep reaching further goals.

The behavior change is for the rest of your life

The reality is that the lifestyle changes you make are for – life. There is no going back without consequence. The upshot, as you will discover, is that if behavior change is implemented the right way, you won't want to go back.

If you are over 40, you are fighting an uphill battle

Our metabolism slows as we age so our body needs fewer calories, plus we have a harder time building and retaining muscle mass and our skin starts to sag. We need to eat right, get regular exercise and not overeat, just to maintain what we have.

Some of us have to work harder than others

Genetics plays a role in our ability to reach our ultimate goals. Understanding and accepting your uniqueness will help you focus clearly on the more important goal of just being healthier and happier.

HOW GOOD DO YOU HAVE TO BE?

With a balanced lifestyle, there is room for pretty much anything. If you need a day to "veg out" on the couch once in a while, that's okay. Need a sweet treat every day? No problem. You won't have to feel guilty about it, but you will have to stay focused on the journey. Success won't magically happen. You still have to put in the effort.

Reflection

Contemplate the following questions to better understand your readiness for change:

- Are you ready to focus on the goal of feeling better and not just losing weight?
- Do you believe that you could become a person who enjoys making healthier choices?
- Are you willing to remove the blinders and keep your eyes open during the journey so you can overcome your obstacles to success?
- Are you willing to accept the realities of lifestyle change?

Accountability, Acknowledgement, Awareness

Blinders keep us from identifying the root of our problems that are sabotaging our efforts to change our behaviors. You can diet with blinders on, but you can't change your lifestyle without open eyes.

To open your eyes, you need to spend some time identifying the underlying obstacles that may be keeping you from change. You may recognize that you are overweight because you eat too much or that you don't get enough exercise, but that can be easily fixed – eat less, exercise more. But it's the why we do what we do, or don't do, that seems to elude most of us and can be the root cause of our inability to succeed.

The chapters in this section will explore some possible mental and environmental barriers that may be keeping you from success. Some areas may apply to you, some not. And, you may discover personal obstacles that aren't even mentioned. You must contemplate, not just read. You may not even be ready to accept some of the realities until you have thought about it for a while. You may want to go back and re-read some chapters while contemplating your own challenges.

The next three chapters will address:

Accountability – Coming clean and accepting responsibility for your actions

Acknowledgment – Paying attention and admitting your actions

Awareness – Becoming aware of what your body wants and needs as the primary reason for making your decisions

While contemplating these chapters, you might want to keep a journal or a note pad and as you go through your day, make a note of when you feel you may be faced with mental obstacles that could be sabotaging your efforts to make good decisions.

That said, you don't have to keep a journal. Why? Because for some of us, required journaling may be an excuse to not read on. "Ugh, I have to keep a journal? Done that before. Forget it." If that is your only obstacle to moving forward, then put the pen down and read on anyway.

5

Accountability: Coming Clean

I speak of the blinders – our eyes being shut and then opened (awakened) a bit only to close again. Closing the blinds has a lot to do with excuses, denial and blame. When we want to close the blinds we make excuses to justify not making good decisions, we will blame someone or some thing for our negative decision, or just deny it ever happened. If you don't know or won't admit to the real reasons you aren't successful, how are you going to overcome them?

Our society makes it easier for us to make excuses, go into denial or to blame. We have made healthy living so complicated and confusing that it's easy to provide an excuse. With our environment being so toxic, it's easy to blame the situation and feel helpless to change. Our lives are so hectic, we don't have time to focus on our problems, so we just go into denial and pretend they aren't happening.

At the initial "getting to know you" visit with a coaching client, I ask them if they are willing to accept responsibility, be honest and accountable for their actions – totally. For some, they stare me right in the eye and say, "YES, I am ready!" and we begin a mutually beneficial journey together. Unfortunately, for others, I see a blank stare in their eyes. They aren't ready to accept responsibility and take the blinders off. They will back pedal and let me know they'll call me later. Then, typically, they will have gone to Jenny Craig or a number of other, less personal ways to lose weight or achieve their goals. And that's okay. I wish them success.

Not being accountable for your actions is typically a huge factor in one's ability to change behaviors. The reality is, you could have the best fitness trainer, a personal chef and all the nutrition knowledge in the world, but if you are wearing blinders and are not accepting responsibility for your negative actions that are at the root of your problem, you will not succeed. To stop excusing, stop blaming and come clean with your current actions – that is, to get out of denial – you must be accountable. Once you are accountable, you can clearly identify what needs to change, and you will be in a better position to take action to do something about it.

Let's talk about some of our actions that keep us unaccountable and unwilling to change our behaviors and think about what actions, if any, may apply to you.

ARE YOU MAKING EXCUSES?

I don't have time. I'm too tired. I was going to but. My knee is acting up again. I wasn't feeling good. I had to do this or that. Anything else but the healthy action you were planning on taking. While sometimes there are valid excuses, most of the time, if you really listen to yourself, you will recognize just how lame many of your excuses are. Until you are ready to stop making excuses, you will not be successful.

Diets and exercise programs give us an excuse to do nothing. Dieting restrictions make it too hard to eat healthy and if your movement has to be timed, structured and measured, then excuses can come easy.

"I don't have time" is always the most popular excuse I hear from my clients. They will insist that they do not have time to fit exercise into their life. They will make "time" excuses day after day, when finally, once they decide to not use time as an excuse, they suddenly find the time. Before they know it, they are taking three mile walks every day just because it makes them feels better – it's something they want to do. So, where did that time come from, when their life really hasn't changed?

PROCRASTINATION

Excuses can sometimes be disguised as procrastination. "I'll exercise, but first I have to . . ." and we procrastinate ourselves into not doing it. Our hectic lives offer a convenient excuse, because there is always something to do or someone else that needs you. As a personal trainer, at times, I was disheartened because many of my clients did not hire me to educate and motivate them to change their lives. Their objective was to put me on the calendar so they would have to be accountable to someone because they weren't able to be accountable to themselves.

Procrastination can be prevented by prioritization. Where are YOU on your list of things to do? While maybe you can't put yourself number one all the time, taking care of you should be in the top three – every day. Taking care of your health, improving the quality of your life and being happier are pretty darn important, don't you think?

Procrastination is also used to delay making good decisions. "I'll start eating right and exercising tomorrow," allow us to not eat well, eat too much, or not move our bodies today. Since lifestyle change is about the immediate reward, not a long-term goal, every decision impacts you now – and not for something that tomorrow brings. For example:

- Choosing an apple over potato chips because it is good for you and won't spoil your dinner

- Pushing your plate away when you are full, so you don't feel stuffed and have regret

- Taking a 10 minute walk when you are feeling lethargic, to revitalize yourself

- Stretching at your desk for two minutes when you're body is feeling stiff, in order to relieve the discomfort

- Taking a meditative cleansing breath when you're in a stressful situation to calm yourself

While you may have good excuses for not carrying out a diet or exercise plan, there are few justifiable excuses for not making hundreds of good decisions that help you feel better along your way.

Pay attention to the excuses you make for not taking a positive lifestyle action. When you find yourself making such an excuse, write it down and then consider what the real reason was for not taking action. Often, the answer is not that the option wasn't available to you, but because of your mental decision not to do it. The truer answer might be:

I made an excuse.

I didn't prioritize.

I procrastinated.

I had blinders on.

I chose not to feel better.

As you progress to lifestyle change, you won't need to rely on excuses because you won't be resistant to it. If you are faced with challenges, you may choose to modify, rather than excuse because the action is important to you.

ARE YOU IN DENIAL?

Denial is, in harsh terms, subconsciously lying to ourselves. Most of us who have struggled with trying to lose a few pounds are guilty of these little white lies that can be so destructive. Some of us do it a little, not a big deal. But for others, it can be the root cause of severe obesity. We go into denial and don't own up to everything we eat, or to other negative actions we take.

Denial is often a culprit in failed weight loss or exercise plans. When we don't follow the rules, we feel that we've cheated, and it's really hard to admit that you are capable of such an unbecoming act.

Honest journaling is a great way to become accountable, which is also why so many people dread it – because they have to be honest with themselves or feel guilty for not admitting the truth. So, in an effort not to fail or cheat, we deny.

Denial is a huge obstacle to the coaching relationship. If I have a client who is unwilling to be honest with me, she is not being honest with herself. There is no point in moving forward, for we will achieve nothing. It becomes a big game where nobody wins.

Could you be guilty of denial? It may be hard to admit, but admitting it is the first step to overcoming the obstacle. It's time to come clean so you can eliminate this destructive obstacle to change. Here are a few examples of denial tactics that may help you identify your own denial actions:

Closet eating

Closet eating is common for those self-conscious about their weight, and can be a primary problem with people who are morbidly obese. They become uncomfortable eating in front of people, so they prefer to eat most of their calories when they are alone. They will bypass taking a piece of birthday cake at a party, only to stop at the bakery on the way home and celebrate alone.

Closet eating has become more of a problem as people try to follow the latest lifestyle practices. They may proclaim that they have become, vegetarian, dairy-free, or all organic and then, when the lifestyle becomes too difficult to practice, they begin sneaking the forbidden foods. While having excellent eating habits is a great thing, if adhering to them is causing you to develop a dysfunctional relationship with food, it's doing more harm than good.

If you are guilty of this destructive behavior, you need to work on having a balanced social relationship with food. Learn to be comfortable eating with others and eliminate or minimize eating done alone. What other people witness or think about how you eat is irrelevant. It's being accountable to yourself that matters.

Not really eating

We subconsciously believe that food eaten without a plate, over the sink, or licked from a spoon doesn't count. I must admit that I've eaten more ice cream out of the container than in a bowl. I'm still famous for "evening out the cake." I've also eaten the equivalent of five Toll House cookies before they even went in the oven. Have you ever been guilty of this? But the calories do count, and you can easily pack on the pounds with this common denial practice.

Selective memory

Many of us can't understand why we aren't successful at weight loss or exercise plans because we claim we follow the plan, but we seem to have selective memory about our actions. We then complain that the program or method didn't work, for example:

"But I do exercise"

Many of us claim that we are avid exercisers, but we are guilty of exaggeration. We may have "gotten into it" for a few weeks or a few months, but over a block of time, it's sporadic at best. We join a gym and say we're going three times a week, but really only go once and then not at all. We buy equipment that collects dust. We show up at an aerobics class once a week, put very little effort into it, and then stop going because we say it wasn't doing anything. If we own equipment, belong to a gym or are enrolled in an exercise class, we claim we are avid exercisers. We just have been a little too busy lately and will "get back into it" soon.

"But I am a healthy eater"

Many of us say we have a healthy diet and do eat healthy foods some of the time, but we are in denial about how much nutritious food we really eat. If we had vegetables with our dinner twice last week and an apple on Tuesday, we claim we are eating healthy. We focus on what we had that was nutritious and forget about how much we ate that wasn't.

Self-sabotage

Without recognizing it, many of us sabotage ourselves in an effort to prove something. This often happens when we are surrounded by naggers or loved ones whose intent is to help us, but are misguided in the delivery of their intentions. When someone asks you "You're not going to eat that, are you?" or "You're getting fat, you need to drop a few pounds," your instinct is to react with a subconscious message of "Don't tell me what to do!" and pushes you to make negative decisions. You may have considered making a good decision on your own, but because someone told you that "you had to," you might do the opposite just to rebel. Most of the time this is done unconsciously – unfortunately, the only one you hurt is yourself.

I find this very common with children, especially teenagers who are most likely to rebel against any parent's wishes. I try to teach parents to empower their children to make decisions on their own through positive reinforcement – let them take ownership of their personal responsibility. I learned this the hard way – through negatively inspiring my own children. Recognizing my misdirected help, I was able to empower them to make better choices for themselves, while I assumed my appropriate role of simply being there as a support system.

THE TRUTH SHALL SET YOU FREE

By not being honest about your actions, you are only hurting yourself. Most of the time it isn't a conscious lie, but a blinder – we really don't see what is or isn't happening. If you don't recognize the action, you can't do anything to change it. Admitting to your actions is the first big step to change. It can be liberating to finally recognize and be accountable for your actions. Come clean and start over.

ARE YOU PLAYING THE BLAME GAME?

Similar to denial, blaming takes the responsibility from ourselves by blaming someone or something else for our inability to be successful or make good decisions. We say we have a slow metabolism, that we are genetically disadvantaged, addicted to carbohydrates, we don't have a turn-off switch in our brain to tell us when we are full, and a host of other new theories to justify the increase in our obesity problem in this country.

Marketing strategies in the food and diet industry like to use the blame game to convince you to use their product. "Poor baby, we understand, let us help you." They always have a reason why you haven't been successful in the past and it is never your fault. They have discovered the answer to your problem and it only costs $19.95.

The big obstacle here is that if you resign yourself to blaming something for your problems, then you will never overcome your situation. If you truly believe you can place the blame on something else, then you have given up. "I can't, because…" guarantees failure.

Here are some realities to consider before you blame:

If your blame is an "addiction" to carbs or sugar:

Do you eat an abundance of fruits, vegetables, lean protein and whole grains along with the excessive amount of empty carbs and sugar? Just because you claim you are addicted to these types of foods doesn't mean you can't also include ample amounts of good food in your stomach as well. Maybe if you did you wouldn't eat as much fat and sugar.

If your blame is a leptin imbalance and you never feel full:

Have you committed to at least get more exercise and eat healthier foods so that you can curtail the damage of your leptin imbalance? If you did, you may still be overweight due to your robust appetite, but at least the foods you eat and the physical activity would offset the negative effects and improve the leptin imbalance.

If your blame is a slow metabolism:

Have you had your thyroid tested? If yes, and it was normal, then your metabolism "condition" is not the problem. Your lifestyle practices are probably at the root of your sluggish metabolism. Are you eating an abundance of fruits, vegetables, lean protein and whole grains, and are you making the effort to get physical activity every day? Are you eating three square meals a day? Maybe if you did, your metabolism wouldn't be so slow.

If your blame is genetics:

You can give yourself some blame credit for body type. Yes, we come in all shapes and sizes and that is a good thing. The world would be pretty boring if we all looked alike. That said, you have to be honest and consider how much is due to genetics and how much to your own actions.

AN INTERESTING STUDY ON THE ROLE OF METABOLISM

There was an amazing study done in the UK on metabolism that got very little publicity, but the findings were interesting. The researchers studied two women who were longtime friends. One was tall and slightly underweight, and the other shorter and 22 pounds overweight. The friends always thought that the tall friend had a faster metabolism and could eat practically anything she wanted and didn't gain weight, while the other friend struggled with a slower metabolism and as a result could not eat as much as her friend.

They both agreed to be tested and closely monitored by scientists and nutritionists for a documentary. Both fasted for 24 hours before having their metabolic rate accurately measured in the lab, using a ventilation hood. They were also told to drink a bottle of special water that would help measure their metabolism. But in fact, it was double-labeled water, which has a non-radioactive isotope marker added to it. This double-labeled water can accurately measure the total amount of calories someone consumes, as well as the total number of calories burned off over a period of time. The scientists didn't reveal the truth about the water because they didn't want the women to be influenced and adjust their normal food intake in any way. This made for much greater accuracy in measuring their normal, everyday food consumption.

The results revealed that over the course of a week both had very similar activity levels, but in fact the heavier friend actually had a higher metabolic rate than the slimmer one! The study also revealed that the heavier friend was in fact consuming about 50 percent more calories than the slimmer one!

What I find most important about this study is not what they found out, but the perception of the two women. Why did both women think that the heavier one had a slower metabolism and ate less? Could it be that the heavier woman was a closet eater, so she didn't appear to eat as much? Did the heavier woman have selective memory? Was the fact that she blamed her metabolism giving her an excuse not to be truthful and face reality?

Be Accountable for Your Actions

You cannot solve your problems if you don't admit you have them. If you think you are guilty of these actions, then it is important that you open your eyes and be accountable for them:

♦ Are you in the habit of making excuses for not making good decisions?

♦ Are you guilty of denial — not admitting your actions?

♦ Have you resigned yourself to blame?

By contemplating these thoughts and actions, you can then identify what's really going on, 'fess up," and work on ways to overcome them.

6

Acknowledgement: It's Not Just What You Eat, But How and Why

*I*f you are relying on excuses, denial and blame for not succeeding in your weight loss goals, you most likely have a few bad eating habits as well. You may try and fail many attempts to lose weight because you are not recognizing your one bad habit – and it just happens to be the one that sabotages your efforts over and over again.

Bad habits have more to do with how and why we eat our food, rather than what we eat. Bad habits go unrecognized partly due to a form of denial that I addressed earlier – selective memory. We seem to forget some things that we ate unintentionally, or won't acknowledge an action that took place.

By uncovering the problem, you can easily tackle the solution. Awareness and acknowledgement of everything you put in your mouth can dramatically reduce the amount of food you eat. By acknowledging every bite, you give yourself a chance to think twice before you make the decision. When we succumb to bad habits, it's the result of us closing the blinds, even just for a minute. And when we open them we don't consciously remember what happened – we have amnesia. Then we wonder why our "diet" isn't working.

Think about it this way. Let's say you have a little bad habit that results in consuming 100 calories more a day that you are not acknowledging. Over the course of a year, if everything you did remained equal, you would have gained 10 pounds!

So rather than focusing on a diet plan, work on a new habit of saying "hello" to everything you are about to put in your mouth, and then make a conscious decision whether to let it in or not. In many cases, the acknowledgement can stop the action.

I was reading a website about stupid patents and came across one I thought wasn't so silly. It was a wristband that sounded an alarm every time you put your hand to your mouth. I didn't think that was so stupid. I thought it was a pretty good idea!

If you can identify and control bad habits, you will eat less. It's a conscious awareness of what you are doing and taking simple steps to change. In order to do this, you have to identify your bad habits and then move towards overcoming them or at least controlling them.

So, here are a few common bad habits that you (and I!) may be guilty of from time to time, and a few ideas to help you overcome them.

DO YOU MINDLESSLY EAT?

You walk in the lunchroom to grab a cup of coffee and walk out with a donut. You weren't hungry, you weren't thinking about eating or craving something sweet; you just saw it and ate it. Three hundred calories of nothing but fat and sugar, leaving you with a bit of indigestion, a temporary sugar rush, and most likely, regret. Most people don't randomly eat a donut and then say, "Gee, I'm so glad I ate that!" We feel guilty, are mad at ourselves for doing it, or even mentally beat ourselves up – overwhelming negative results from a two-second mindless decision. Or, we go into denial and never admit we ate it.

You are in the kitchen when your kids come home from school. They are pulling out the Doritos, cookies or other snack. And as you ask them about their day, you slip your hand into the bag, remove a few and chomp away. Then your hand quietly slips in again, once, maybe twice or more – a cookie here, a chip there, but it goes unrecognized. An hour later, you sit down to dinner with your Lean Cuisine, proud of yourself for being so good! What you may not realize is that your little bout of mindless eating could be more calories than your dinner, and you didn't even enjoy or acknowledge the food you ate.

Sound familiar? If so, here are a few tips to help you overcome mindless eating:

Don't eat while standing up

Mindless eating is often done while standing. We graze by the kitchen counter or our coworker's desk, grab a sweet treat and pop it into our mouth without so much as a small acknowledgement. Learn to sit down and pay attention to the fact that you are eating. If you decide to put your hand in the cookie jar at least sit down, acknowledge it and enjoy it.

Control ravenous eating

Do you have a habit of walking through the door after work, starving, rummage through the kitchen eating everything in sight, and then sit down and eat dinner? This is a typical bad habit of people who don't eat regularly. They eat little during the day to be "good," and then break down and mindlessly eat while preparing dinner, consuming excess calories that were neither enjoyed nor acknowledged. So, the calories they should have eaten throughout the day are ravenously eaten along with their dinner, resulting in excess calories, unbalanced eating and weight gain. If you need something in your stomach before dinner, choose something light that can stave off hunger without ruining your dinner. If you are a conscious eater, you will stop and consider if you want to lose the enjoyment of sitting down to a nice dinner because of a three-minute food binge. My saviors are baby carrots. I nosh on them while preparing dinner – just a few calories, a good crunch and I get extra veggies in my diet as an added bonus! If you don't like carrots, try peppers, celery or a cut-up apple instead.

Keep food less accessible

Food that is on the counter or on your desk is easier to mindlessly eat than if you keep it in a drawer or hidden in a closet. Out of sight, out of mind.

Don't be afraid to waste food

Do you deposit the last handful of stale cereal in your mouth before you throw out the box, chew up the crusts off your kids' sandwich, or eat the last glob of mashed potatoes while doing the dishes? We were always taught to never waste food – after all, there are people starving in Africa! And that was a pretty good rule in the old days, when the food we ate was mostly used to nourish us and not as readily available. The problem today is, most of the food we won't waste is not nutritious. If you are overweight and unhealthy, and you choose to put excess food in your stomach rather than a trash can, it is still wasteful. Your stomach is the trash can, which is worse because what you're tossing into it is harming you.

An interesting observation is that many of us will be reluctant to throw away the remainder of a cheap birthday cake that we have been uncontrollably picking at while trying to lose weight. Yet, we have no problem throwing away $12 worth of rotted, uneaten vegetables and fruit from the produce drawer.

Don't eat what you don't want

Unless you are starving and it's the only thing available, don't eat food that is not appealing to you. For example, the soggy fries at the bottom of the fast food bag – do they really taste good? Or are you just eating them because they are French fries, and greasy, fatty junk food is supposed to taste good, so we eat them without even stopping to think about whether or not the taste is appealing to us.

An example of how I save many calories a day is to have a discriminating palate. For example, if I am eating one of those huge restaurant wraps, which typically are loaded with calories, I will tear off the excess dough. Not necessarily to save the calories, but because it can make the sandwich taste gummy and camouflage the good flavors inside. Think about how every bite tastes and if the food is just adding extra calories you don't need then don't eat it.

Bottom line is, don't put any food in your mouth unless you have acknowledged it. Be selective with the food you choose to eat, sit down and enjoy it.

DO YOU EAT TOO FAST?

Emily Post would turn over in her grave if she saw the way we eat today. We gobble our food, talk with our mouths full and have bad table manners. Years ago we were taught to keep our elbows off the table, only cut three pieces of meat at a time, put our knives down, and chew our food. Many of us have loosened the rules of table etiquette and our children can be especially terrible. One of my clients revealed that her ten-year-old son refused to eat with utensils and ate only with his hands.

The type of food we eat has also impacted how we eat. Many convenience foods are eaten with our hands, especially large sandwiches. We tend to hold onto them, never putting the sandwich down. We work any conversation in while moving the sandwich to the side and then continue to munch away until it's gone. Some of these sandwiches are almost 1000 calories and we are downing them in minutes.

Eating too fast causes overeating, which causes weight gain – and it can cause a lot of weight gain. Many times we overeat because the enjoyment of eating the food is over too fast and we want more because we aren't mentally satisfied.

Eating slower can reduce your caloric intake without much effort because you experience the same taste pleasure with less consumption. Also, by eating slower, your body has time to acknowledge it's full and you will reach the same satisfaction level with less food.

Have you considered how you eat? Here's an experiment. The next time you have a meal, pay attention to how you are eating. When you swallow, is there so much food going down that it feels lumpy in your throat? Is the next bite or forkful in your mouth ready to follow? At the same time, are you ready to shovel in still another?

Now, try eating slower. How do you do that? Put less food on your fork or take smaller bites. Chew your food more so that when you swallow, it feels more comfortable. Then, take another bite after you swallow. One forkful is digested before the next forkful comes in. If you are eating with someone, stop the process, put the fork or food down while talking, and don't talk with your mouth full!

Eating slower takes practice. If you find yourself "wolfing down" food, stop the action. If you keep reminding yourself to slow down, eventually you will naturally start eating slower and you will enjoy your food more. It really works!

ARE YOU OVEREATING?

How much are you eating? Probably more than you think. While food should be enjoyed, every meal should not be a special occasion to overeat. In today's overfed world we do not recognize the difference between being full versus being stuffed. We have lost touch with what "normal" eating is and are consistently eating more calories than our bodies need. Many of us are on a constant weight-gaining track.

People who don't have weight issues simply don't eat too much. They eat until they are content. How many times do you finish eating and are not satisfied, but uncomfortable. Now, if it's Thanksgiving or that special night out (once a month, not three times a week), that's okay. But if you are feeling this way on a regular basis, then you are chronically overeating and you will gain weight. And, you most likely aren't feeling very well.

The habit of eating until you are uncomfortable keeps the pharmaceutical companies busy by taking care of all of our "acid reflux" ailments. It's an awareness of what is going on with our bodies that needs to come into play. Here are some ideas to help:

Stop eating

If you are eating too much, just stop. I know what you're thinking, "It tastes too good to stop!" Often overeating goes hand-in-hand with eating too fast. Most of us don't recognize we are full because we are eating too fast and aren't giving ourselves enough time to listen to our bodies to let us know if we are full. If it tastes so good, then why are we in such a hurry to eat it? If you eat it slowly and savor the sights, smells and tastes of your food, isn't that enough enjoyment? During the eating process, stop every few minutes, take a deep breath, look at your food and consider what your body is feeling. Think about whether your mind is at work or your body. How will you feel afterward if you keep eating? Will you be sluggish? Will you be uncomfortable and suffer from indigestion? Will you mentally beat yourself up? Take a second to ask yourself, "Do I really want this?"

Eat in the moment

Overeating can occur when we don't acknowledge and enjoy the food that we are eating at that moment. Acknowledge that it is time to eat and enjoy your time with it. Sometimes, while we're eating what's on our plate, we are anticipating what we are going to eat next. It's like the purpose of eating what's on our plate is so that we can have some more!

Don't multi-task your eating

With our hectic schedules many times we eat while doing other things, which can be a distraction. You aren't eating in the moment and you aren't recognizing the fullness in your stomach. So even though you may be full, you feel cheated because you haven't had the experience and enjoyment of eating.

Walk away for a minute

If you are tempted to have the second helping, another cookie, etc. and can't seem to resist, instead of saying, "No you can't," make a deal with yourself. Walk away and do something constructive with the option to return and eat some more. Often, you may find the distraction will lessen the strong urge to eat more.

Don't keep food in front of you

When eating informally, don't put the food on the table. Have the family fix a plate and bring it to the table. It takes more effort and thought to get up from the table and get a second helping. Also, if it's in front of you, then you are more likely to pick at it.

Overeat on the good stuff

If you enjoy the action of eating, then expand your eating enjoyment with food that is good for you and lower in calories. Add more veggies on your plate and you will be able to eat longer with less damage and better nutrition.

Measure out snacks

The 100-calorie packs are very popular, and with good reason. But you don't have to pay the extra cost of packaging – just measure out a serving in a dish or in plastic bags. A problem with the convenience packs is that you don't learn how much a serving really is, so it doesn't teach you control. If you measure out your own, then you know how much to take when you can't rely on the 100-calorie pack.

Trick yourself

Sometimes the action is more important than the actual food you are eating. For example, you have a lifelong habit of going for seconds at meals. If you are having trouble conquering this lifelong habit, try tricking yourself by taking smaller first helpings (or use a smaller plate). Then allow yourself a second, smaller helping, acknowledging that you can always go back for more. But with smaller helpings, you have to actually make a decision to go back for thirds and are probably less likely to do it.

Avoid distractions

Try to avoid TV, reading or hot issue conversation when eating. These distractions can keep you from acknowledging what you are eating and keep you from recognizing the enjoyment or experience of eating your food. If you are engrossed in a serious conversation, your stress level may rise, causing you to eat faster as well.

Eat more from home

Suffice it to say, a big culprit in overeating is eating out at restaurants, which most of us do on a regular basis. Let me assure you that if you go out to eat, most likely you are overeating. Most chain restaurants entrées have 50-100 percent of the daily-recommended calorie, fat and sodium requirements. Add to it a basket of bread and a drink – not to mention an appetizer or dessert – and you are gluttonously overeating. It is necessary for you to cut back on this behavior in order for you to have balanced eating. Just one or two excursions a week such as this can sabotage any positive effort you put into weight loss, and will most likely cause ongoing weight gain. Later in the book I will provide some tips on how to eat at restaurants without being gluttonous.

Overeating is typically caused by eating so fast that the stomach doesn't have time to tell the brain it's full. Meanwhile, the brain is in a state of eating frenzy and isn't aware of what the body is consuming. You aren't in a state of enjoyment of food, so you aren't mentally satisfied with the event. By paying attention to what you are eating, you can eliminate overeating without mental sacrifice.

ARE YOU AN EMOTIONAL EATER?

In our stress-crazed world, many of us fall victim to emotional or stress eating. It's our comfort, our reward – a baby bottle. I think most of us are guilty of emotional eating from time to time. But for some of us, the habit can have huge repercussions. People who are morbidly obese typically have an emotional eating problem, and the condition is spreading as more food is available and stress increases.

There are many great books that address the issues of emotional eating, which can be a huge barrier to successful weight loss and finding balance. My purpose is not to address what is causing your emotional eating issues, but to help you become more conscious of their existence. If you recognize that emotional eating is a big problem for you that you cannot overcome on your own, then I highly recommend you explore your issues further and get help.

What's really going on when we eat emotionally? Typically, it's a trancelike experience. We put our blinders on and sort of go into a conscious coma, relieving ourselves from the stresses of the world by wallowing in calories – typically fat-laden empty calories. It seems that when we feel stressed or depressed, we look to sabotage ourselves even more by being self-destructive. So is it an uncontrollable condition? Or is it simply a bad habit? I think for the majority of us, it's a habitual reaction that can be minimized with accountability, awareness and acknowledgement. The reality is, most people try to combat this type of eating by going on a diet, which is unproductive because it doesn't address the issue. If you are struggling with your weight and you know you are an emotional eater, then you need to work on the whys and actions that take place, not find another way to lose weight. By allowing, analyzing and redirecting your actions, you can become your own therapist and you may be capable of eliminating or at least controlling the damage it causes. Here are a few things to think about that might help:

Consider the inevitable regret

When going for the binge decision, think about the impact regret may have on you later. How are you going to feel, not for the five minute relief, but for the hours – maybe even days – afterward? Guilt and regret trigger emotional eating. Emotional eating triggers guilt and regret. It's a vicious cycle that can be very destructive. Keeping the blinds open by being aware of the inevitable regret when making an emotional eating decision might help you break the cycle.

Find a better way to relieve stress

When you recognize the immediate repercussion of your negative action, you can consider more productive stress relieving options that will result in a positive outcome. For instance, going for a walk, eating a relaxing, healthy dinner, talking to a friend, having sex or taking a bath. Before diving in, ask yourself, "Do I want to feel better?" If your goal is to productively, not destructively, deal with your stress, you can change your choices.

Minimize the damage

But it's not always that easy. Sometimes, when we ask ourselves "Do I want to feel better?" The only answer we find is "No." The urge to seek comfort in food can be overwhelming. Typically, it's not really the food, but the emotional action that we crave. It's very strange, but when we feel sad or stressed, for some reason we just don't want to feel better and actually choose to make ourselves feel worse.

So, maybe it is okay to sometimes allow yourself to emotionally eat from time to time. If you are aware that you are about to emotionally eat, you can minimize the damage and make it more constructive. Here's kind of a weird, but helpful example: Say, you want to bury yourself in a container of ice cream and a large spoon. This action could result in 600-800 calories and a lot of regret. Instead, take a dish of ice cream and focus on looking at the food more than eating it. Stir it around, play with it, eat it slowly. As you are enjoying the relief of the moment, think about what is stressing you out, what effect it is having on you, and what steps you can take to make the situation better.

If you cannot control your emotional eating and it is interfering with your happiness, then do yourself a favor and seek counseling.

Emotional eating can be very debilitating and can have deep roots. Life is too short not to take steps to overcome the damage it may be having on the quality of your life.

ARE YOU A LATE NIGHT EATER?

There is a myth that eating late at night causes weight gain. While that is not really true, when you are tired, you are more vulnerable to overeating and picking. Your willpower diminishes because you are too tired to fight your temptations and make good decisions. Save yourself by changing some habits to keep you from being so vulnerable.

Close the kitchen

The open kitchen/family room floor plans cause us to hang out in the kitchen late into the night. Try to give yourself a rule that you cannot re-enter the kitchen area after, say, 8:00 pm.

Go to bed earlier

Even if you don't plan to "sleep," at least get settled in, read a book, take a bath or watch TV. Most of us do not get enough sleep and could benefit by an earlier routine.

Eat dinner early

With our busy lifestyles, sometimes we don't relax to eat dinner until much later at night. But, in the meantime, we've consumed a lot of unhealthy calories to tie us over. Say lunch is at 12:00, but dinner isn't until 8:00. So, from 4:00 to 8:00 we might consume hundreds of extra calories. Typically, in unhealthy choices like cookies, chips, or whatever might be available but we don't consider these extra calories when we sit down to our actual dinner. Try to arrange your schedule so that you can have an earlier dinner time. Combine this routine with an earlier bedtime and you can reduce a lot of unwanted calories, your body will be more settled and you will feel better.

DO YOU EAT ON THE RUN?

Even if you aren't generally a fast eater, eating on the run instigates faster eating, which leads to eating too much. Most often, the foods we eat on the run come from the drive-thru and are generally high calorie and low-nutrition foods. The other day I saw a guy in his car with a Big Mac in one hand, while driving his car with the other. He's eating a 500-calorie sandwich (most likely with a 400-calorie bag of fries at his side) and his eating "pleasure" is over before he gets to the next intersection. If you are on the run and get hungry, find something that can just calm down your hunger cravings. Nutrition bars are a great choice. You can keep them in your glove compartment for emergencies. While they aren't the tastiest food, they do help stave off your appetite until you are ready to sit down and enjoy a meal.

SUCCESS DOESN'T HAPPEN OVERNIGHT

Getting rid of bad habits doesn't happen overnight. Expect that you aren't always going to be successful. If you have been practicing a habit for years, it will not be easily broken. It will take time, but if you consistently acknowledge your actions, you will get better results and making good decisions will become easier.

Work on identifying and controlling any bad habit you have, and you will be on your way to weight loss and better health. At the same time you will enjoy the food you eat even more. Get into a better habit of stopping and asking yourself why you are eating and if you are enjoying it. Sit down, say "hello" to what you are about to eat, and enjoy!

Acknowledge What You Eat

Every time you go to put something in your mouth, ask yourself:

- ◆ Do I really want this?
- ◆ Is it better off in the garbage than in my mouth?
- ◆ Will it spoil my next meal?
- ◆ How am I eating? Am I eating too fast?
- ◆ Why am I eating if I'm not even hungry?
- ◆ How will I feel moments after I eat it and is it worth it?

Awareness: What Does Your Body Really Want?

We've talked about the mental obstacles that could keep you from change or sabotage your efforts. And, the practices of acknowledgement and accountability for your actions that may get you on your way to weight loss and better health. In this chapter, we are going to talk about how to become aware of what it is your body wants and needs, and how to avoid being distracted by our environment, our negative influences and our mind games.

I made the claim earlier that you would be able to eat what you want and still lose weight. That most likely sounded like the same rhetoric you hear on endless product commercials. Logically, we should know that if we are not responsible for everything we eat and sit on our butts, we shouldn't expect to lose weight and be healthy. However, that is what many of us blindly expect. We keep hoping for that magic bullet that will allow us to have everything we want, not change a thing, and still lose weight and be healthy.

I also talked about becoming one of "those" people – the ones who seem to always maintain their weight and are physically active, but don't seem to consider it a sacrifice or a big deal. It's not that they are necessarily more disciplined and have more will power. Eating moderately and moving their bodies is something they "want" to do, so these decisions aren't difficult to make. Wanting to do something is easier than having to do something, right? So, let's talk about how you can change your desire for decisions that have negative outcomes for ones that result in better outcomes.

THINK DIFFERENTLY

Typically, when we try to change our habits, we expect ourselves to just flip a switch and transform our thinking. We try to modify our habits too quickly and then it becomes a sacrifice. We try to give up what we want and aren't consistent in our efforts. With so much working against us, we can only rely on will power and discipline to succeed. When we give into our weaknesses, we eventually put up blinders and rely on excuses, denial and blame to relieve ourselves of the guilt.

Changing our habits and our thinking about what we want is a gradual process. It's slowly adapting to changes, shifting the reasoning behind your actions and recognizing the positive impact it has on you. It's developing the desire to want the positive changes so much that you make the right decision. It's thinking about living in a totally different way so that you can actually want to make better decisions without sacrifice or a lot of will power.

LISTENING TO YOUR BODY

When we aren't one of "those," people we tend to be narrowly focused. The primary drivers of our decisions might be the five minutes of tasty eating or, in the case of diet driven people, the thought that healthy eating, moving our body or having to stop eating is a sacrifice. These thought processes don't have anything to do with giving your body what it wants and needs.

Deciding what you put in your mouth and whether or not you choose to move starts in the brain. But, the reaction and outcome of those decisions impacts the body. By listening to confusing information and being resistant to move, we have been using our mind to make all our decisions without consulting our body. If you can consider and recognize what your body wants and needs first, then it will be easier for you to make the right decision.

Let me explain what I mean by shifting your thinking about what you want and adopting changes to become one of "those" people. The following sections might help you understand this subtle transformation and think differently when making decisions for a healthier outcome.

ACCEPTING OUR RESPONSIBILITY

Somewhere along the line, we stopped accepting responsibility for our actions, exasperated by the irresponsible way our society has been transformed. Eating out, eating unhealthy foods, overeating, not being physically active – it's a way of life for most Americans. Since the irresponsible behavior is normal, we don't really recognize that we are being irresponsible – it's more like "Gosh, I can't eat what everyone else eats because I need to lose weight." The reality is, if you choose to follow the course of excessively eating unhealthy foods and not moving your body, you will be overweight and you may eventually have side effects like diabetes, high cholesterol, depression, sleep apnea, and a load of other health problems. We need to start taking responsibility for our actions because our survival may depend on it. Once you recognize this and stop resisting because you feel like you are being denied, your mind will respond accordingly. Making better decisions will become easier because you will have a healthier, realistic mindset.

We have to realize that eating foods that provide us with the nutrients we need to be healthy and eating in moderation shouldn't be a sacrifice. This is what we are supposed to do. We need to get a grip on this reality and stop whining and start behaving respectfully toward our bodies and our lives. If you don't accept this, don't expect things to change. Make a decision. Do you want to lose weight, be healthy, feel better and have a better quality of life? Or not? If you do, then you must change your behaviors in spite of what's going on around you, and to get there you must change what you eat, how much you eat and how often you move. While it's always nice to have a decadent meal or sit on the cozy couch, you have a responsibility to take care of yourself as well. The part many don't understand is that living this way is more fun, it's fulfilling and you simply feel better for it.

ADAPTING TO BETTER BEHAVIORS PATIENCE IS A VIRTUE

Being impatient instigates failure. We wake up and want to lose 20 pounds and think we are just going to go from a fat loving, junk food eating, couch potato to an all natural, no sugar, yoga lover overnight. We are determined to adhere to a strict diet and exercise program with sheer will power and set off on a race to "get 'er done," which inevitably doesn't last more than a week, a day or even half a day. As I said before, to have a balanced life forever, you have to like it. It can't be a sacrifice, or you will always be looking forward for it all to end.

If you allow yourself time to adapt to changes and not feel as if you are relying on will power to make decisions, the gradual changes you make will become a new way of life. What you used to think was a sacrifice becomes something you want to do, not have to do. Remember, it's not about the race to lose weight or be healthier. It's about the journey, the transformation of what you want, and how you want to live your life.

SHIFTING YOUR FOCUS

When making choices as to what to eat, most of us think about taste, which is important. After all, we all want to enjoy eating. But before you make that decision, you must also consider that the main reason you eat is for nourishment. When thinking, "Do I want something sweet, fatty or salty?", you must also consider whether your body has had enough nutrition. If not, then make that decision first, or in combination with your decision on taste. The problem is that most people think of the nutrition part as just something we are told we have to do, so we are immediately resistant to it. If you want to give your body what it wants and needs and accept responsibility for it, the shift in thinking can make a huge difference in your ability to make better choices. If you make the effort to do this, after a while you will start to crave the nutritious foods as well. So, when thinking about what you want to eat, the nutritious foods become part of the decision. While before you might have instinctively gone for the Doritos or a cookie, if you haven't had enough vegetables that day, you start to consider, "Hmm, I think I want a carrot."

Likewise, when making decisions on moving our bodies, we think of the effort as something negative. Remember when you were a kid you'd fidget through class, looking out the window in anticipation of RECESS! We lived for the opportunity just to run around in circles. Instead of being resistant to exercise, think of it as a savored opportunity for movement. After all, we've got to sit all day – wouldn't it be great to have 10 minutes to get up and give ourselves recess?

CHANGE WHAT IT MEANS TO BE GOOD TO YOURSELF

I was making some whole grain pancakes one winter weekend morning after a great brisk walk with my husband and dogs. As I was looking out the window waiting for the "flip," I was balancing on one leg, and extending the other, just for the fun of it. Focusing on the pleasant feeling of my actions, I was thinking, "How can I get people to understand this?" At one point in my life, my weekend mornings meant a trip to McDonalds for Egg McMuffins followed by a swing by Dunkin' Donuts for a dozen and the morning paper, only to find myself a half hour later on the couch, feeling sluggish, stuffed and regretfully thinking, "Ugh, why did I do that again?" My life is so much happier now – I would never want to go back to those days again, even if it meant I wouldn't gain a pound.

The reality is, I can't just tell you to do this and then it just magically happens. But, as a Lifestyle Coach, I have helped people discover this transition of thinking over a period of time – helped them gradually adjust and awaken to this changed focus. If you are willing to be patient, make gradual changes and be open to the possibility that you can transition your thinking, you might be able to successfully coach yourself to change what you want. If you take small steps to gradually change your behaviors and not think of it as a sacrifice, you can completely change what it means to be good to yourself.

TASTE ADAPTATION

If you have an unhealthy diet and/or are overweight, you are either eating too much fat, sugar or a combination of both. With today's increasing obesity problem, we have been referring to one's excessive desire for fat and/or sugar as an addiction. While I would not boldly say that this is a myth, I strongly suggest that it's simply an acquired taste for most of us – especially when it comes to fat. Since our consumption of fatty foods has increased, so has our palate for it. The more cheese, butter or frying, the better – which has devastating results. Some theories say the answer is to "give it up," which is really, really hard to do because you are giving up something you love.

The simple solution is to slowly reduce the amount of fat and sugar in your diet and allow your palate to adjust. Transitioning without sacrifice. It isn't the fastest way. But let's be reminded that the goal is forever so we don't have a timetable.

So, if your weakness is cheese, simply ask for less cheese, which is pretty easy. As your palate adjusts, scale back a little more. Do this consistently and, over time, you will find that something fried or dripping in cheese is not as appealing to you any more. Or at least it becomes easier to make the healthier decision. Don't believe it? Ask people who used to be fast food junk eaters who now prefer eating lower fat, healthier foods (including me). They will tell you that they aren't interested in fatty foods because they don't enjoy eating them any more. On occasion, I might eat an onion ring or two when they are hot and crunchy, but they lose their appeal very quickly – especially when they get cold and limp – yuck! If you discover that the effects of eating fatty foods are indigestion, a pasty mouth, bad breath and feeling more sluggish , then it's a bit easier to resist.

Sugar is an acquired taste as well. To illustrate an example of how taste adaptation works, try this. Eat a spoonful of light fruit yogurt. Now have something really sweet (like a piece of candy) and take another bite of the yogurt. You will find that the yogurt tastes sour because your taste perspective has changed. If you start the morning with a donut, then your palate will crave this type of food for the rest of the day – even though your body may be craving protein, fruits or vegetables.

Changing your palate does take time, but if it's not a sacrifice then you are less likely to be resistant to it. Give it time and think positively about it. Learn to enjoy the feeling of better nutrition.

ADAPTING TO HEALTHIER FOODS

Most of us who have a sustained healthier lifestyle eat fruits and vegetables, choose whole grains over white flour, and limit our fat and sugar because we prefer it instead of the alternative. Making healthier decisions just happens. If you currently eat very little produce and feel more satisfied with fat and sugar, you may not be able to comprehend changing those preferences. But you can and, as I said before, millions of people have done it and most of them probably had thought the same thing.

To help you adjust to healthier foods, eat them with a different mindset. Consider that by making the healthier choices, you are doing something good for your body. You may not love the taste of broccoli and prefer to leave it on your plate, but if you just eat it anyway and do so with an open mind, aware that by eating it you are doing something good for yourself, that alone can stimulate your senses to appreciate the taste more.

Everything we put in our body does not have to fulfill our entertainment need. It goes back to the old rules when you couldn't leave the table without eating your vegetables. You were being taught that even though it might not be your first preference, you needed them anyway so you ate them. Instead of denying yourself certain foods you enjoy in lieu of healthier foods, simply start by adding healthier foods to your repertoire of everyday food without the pre-set thinking of it being a sacrifice. And, most importantly, eat the healthier foods first – sort of your responsibility before your entertainment. By choosing them positively, you might soon find that you may actually prefer them. The end result may be that after you eat the healthier foods, your body is satisfied and the unhealthy foods start to change their appeal.

VISUAL ADAPTATION

There are few things more enticing than a fancy cake – especially for someone who loves sweets. But even though it may look good, does it actually taste good? Sometimes yes, often no. Before you indulge too much, stop to consider the taste. Could it be dry, overly sweet or plastic tasting – does it really taste as good as you visualized it? How much are your eyes at work, rather than your palate, let alone your stomach?

Just like taste adaptation, through the change process, you can experience visual adaptation. As you change your eating habits, rather than looking at the hot pizza out of the oven as "yummy" you might instead notice the grease sitting on top of it, or the excessive cheese dripping off of it and find it not so appealing. Instead, you may look at the colorful basket of fruits and vegetables as enticing. Now don't get me wrong, sometimes a piece of pizza can be appealing even if you are a healthy eater (And it sure smells good!), but only in moderation, and only after you've had your fill of more nutritious foods. Pizza actually is not a terribly unwholesome food. The problem is most pizza served today is grossly fatty, so if you learn to have a taste adaptation for less fatty foods and enjoy pizza, simply remove the excess cheese and enjoy!

ADAPTING TO A LEVEL PLAYING FIELD

Consider this: What if all food had the same amount of calories and nutritional value? What if there were no good food, bad food, can have, can't have? Would that impact your decisions? Probably so. Could you imagine being offered an array of goodies, like brownies, cake, French fries or a plate of roasted vegetables, and happily choosing the vegetables without temptation? People who have a balanced lifestyle and listen to their bodies don't view food as either good or evil, so the playing field is level. It doesn't matter if one is laden with luscious fat and sugar while the other is low in calories and nutritious. If they are craving vegetables, they'll choose the vegetables. If they have a sweet tooth, they may choose a brownie. If they naturally eat a balance of foods, the decision isn't a big deal. That leaves them the freedom of choice, without mind games, to make decisions on what will make them feel better or satisfy their body's cravings.

Since society is so caught up in the diet mentality we have an angel-devil stream of consciousness. We know we are supposed to choose the chicken and vegetables, but we can't resist the temptation of the four-cheese Fettuccine Alfredo – our evil self. We might sit at the restaurant with our guests and decide as a group "Oh, what the heck, let's be bad!" And there is a feeling of excitement, for a moment. Then when we are done, it's not so exciting any more. The guilt sets in, the realization of what we have done eventually shows up on the scale, and we have regrets. Not only will we have regrets on the scale, but more importantly, we have immediate regrets as to how we feel – indigestion, uncomfortable, sluggish.

So, is the five minutes of gluttonous pleasure worth the hours of indigestion and being uncomfortable? In the end, are you glad you made the Alfredo decision. If you had to do it again, would you make a different decision? How good did the Alfredo really taste when you consider all the negative outcomes of that decision? Maybe what your body really wanted was the healthier option, but you let your devil consciousness take over.

ADAPTING TO YOUR FULLNESS LEVEL

Weight gain comes from eating more calories than your body needs over a long period of time. People who are struggling with their weight typically have a habit where they don't stop eating until their fullness level goes beyond what the body wants – their mental reaction to food takes priority over their body's reaction. The eating process doesn't stop until we reach a level of discomfort. The discomfort level has many degrees. It could mean just a few bites more or, in the case of obesity, we don't stop until we can't eat any more or we will be sick. Your body's signals have to scream at you before you pay attention.

Without influence, your body will tell you when it's full. The problem is, we have been doing so much overeating that we don't know when our bodies are telling us to stop. We are so used to being stuffed after we eat that we think it's normal. If you finish eating and your stomach is uncomfortable, you're belching a lot, you want to unbutton your pants, and you say out loud, "Why do I feel so stuffed?" or "I shouldn't have eaten all of that" . . . We know when we've overeaten – we just choose not to stop. So, in many cases, the difference between fullness and regret could be as little as a minute or two, one or two fewer bites, or just stopping to take a breath. If you start to focus on wanting the regret less than the few extra bites, and not feeling that putting the fork down is a sacrifice, it is easier to make the decision to stop eating before you've eaten too much.

As you adapt to your new lifestyle, focus not on the fact that you have to stop eating when you don't want to, but instead become mindful of how your body feels in the moment. Eating slowly and paying attention to your food helps. You have time to acknowledge your body's reaction to the food you are eating and to recognize when it needs to stop. If you eat in the moment, enjoying the taste and the mental and visual satisfaction, you will be better able to allow your body time to tell you it's had enough. This is a conscious act and needs to be practiced until it becomes natural to you.

SHRINKING STOMACH

Some say it is a myth that when you eat less your stomach shrinks. While it is a myth that the size of your stomach actually does shrink, it is true for most of us that when we start eating less, we get full faster. Unfortunately, once we start overeating again we want to eat more all over again. When we are on restrictive diets and we always want more but just can't have it, our goal is to go back to our old habits once we are off the diet. Whether we are hungry or not isn't a big factor in the process. If you are not on a diet, you can listen to your body and determine that you just aren't hungry any more and you contentedly don't eat more.

When trying to adjust your fullness level, think of "shrinking your stomach" as a virtual gastric stapling. Doctors surgically make your stomach smaller so you can't eat more without severe medical consequences. When transforming your food quantity thinking, visualize your stomach as smaller and that when you are overly full you will have consequences – you will be uncomfortable, sluggish, gain weight and, if you overeat to the point of abuse, it could be dangerous to your health.

THE LESS YOU MOVE, THE LESS YOU WANT TO MOVE

With our sedentary lifestyles, most of us are not just resistant to exercise we have become resistant to the mere act of moving. We actually go out of our way to not move. Something that should be natural to us has become a big effort. With 150 channels on our TV, TIVO, computers, video games and modern conveniences, moving our bodies has become optional. But that doesn't change the fact that our bodies are meant to move in order to be healthy and to feel good. Just as our bodies have adapted to a sedentary lifestyle, they can gradually adapt back to an active lifestyle. Commonly, when we have a sedentary lifestyle, we try to jump back into being active by immediately exerting ourselves way beyond what we are accustomed to – like joining a gym or participating in intense or long duration aerobic activity. The effort is such a jolt that it becomes overwhelming and too difficult and we become resistant to it.

By contrast, if you increase activity gradually, you are able to appreciate the movement and will have time to notice how much better you feel. It isn't a sacrifice and you can eventually become a more active person again, because you want to do it. There are many easy ways to get you started to adapting to a more active lifestyle. We will talk more about it in *Chapter 11 – Just Get Up and Do Something!*

Be Aware of What Your Body Wants

In today's world, making decisions about our lifestyle is influenced by our unhealthy social standards and our dieting sacrifice mindset. We don't consider first what our bodies want and need, which should be our primary consideration. Your body will tell you what it wants and needs to be healthy and balanced. To help yourself listen to your body's wants and not your mind, try gradually adapting to the following changed thinking and listening:

- ◆ Accept responsibility for taking care of your body
- ◆ Be patient and consistent with your changes
- ◆ Practice gradual adaptation of taste and fullness
- ◆ Consider how your body will feel after you have made your mental decision
- ◆ View all food as equal
- ◆ Learn to appreciate moving your body more as a reward, not a punishment

Designing Your Balanced Lifestyle Plan

Once you have contemplated mental obstacles that have been keeping you from change, you can move forward with designing your lifestyle plan. By following the principles of moderation and balance you will be able to eat, move and live in a way that works best for you – one that you can enjoy for the rest of your life.

In order for most diet programs to work, you have to follow their plan – their restrictions, good food, bad food, can have, can't have. It is not only difficult to lose weight this way; it's even more difficult to maintain it. It can be very hard to follow these rules and fit them into your life. Diets assume you are incapable of making decisions for yourself, and so they make them for you. Exercise programs require you to set up a specific schedule, go to a gym or make some other commitment that may be difficult for you to honor. What we are going to learn is how to get educated in the basics so you can choose your own food, physical activity and life management plan to find your personal balance.

For most of us, our choices have been inspired by the out of balance world we live in, and this has consequences. Here are some important factors that are influencing our negative lifestyle behaviors:

♦ Society views gluttonous and lethargic behaviors as normal, and balanced behaviors as sacrifice

♦ We are coerced into eating "fake" food but don't eat enough real food, particularly fruits and vegetables

♦ The food we eat consists of primarily fat and/or sugar and the portion sizes are ridiculous

♦ We don't prepare our food from, or eat at, home, so we are not in control of what goes into our food

♦ Moving our bodies is optional

♦ Our lives are so busy we let everyone and everything get in the way of our needs

We have either forgotten, or really have never known, when moderation and balance was the typical American way of life, or when we made choices in a responsible way. In this section, we are going to help you think about what foods you might eat for balance and how much food you would eat for moderation. We will also address some of the popular myths and unfounded theories that might be confusing you.

Rather than provide you with technical information on how much, how long or at what intensity you should exercise for optimum health, we will spend some time motivating you to simply move your body more and learn to enjoy doing it. And, since stress has become a player in our inability to lead a better quality of life, we'll help you identify stressors in your life and the potential negative impact they may be having on you.

The next four chapters will address these areas:

♦ Eating Right: It's Simple, But It Got Complicated

♦ Realities of Weight Loss

♦ Just Get Up and Do Something

♦ Be Aware of Your Stress

Then I will provide you with stories of people who have identified their obstacles to change and found their balance.

Implementing a moderate and balanced lifestyle is not difficult. The success of your balanced lifestyle plan will depend on the effort you put into it. Your first objective should be to move towards healthier behaviors. If you choose to go beyond this and discipline yourself to do more so you can get into your bikini or run that 10K, then you will already have the foundation to do so.

Eating Right: It's Simple, But It Got Complicated

*W*hile science has come a long way toward understanding the complexities of food and its effect on the body, it has done little to actually educate us on a better way to eat – in fact, our eating habits have gotten worse. We have put foods under a microscope and individually labeled them as good for us or bad for us, healthy or unhealthy. Instead, food consumption should be looked at as a whole – everything we eat over a span of time. By isolating food values we are limiting and depriving ourselves and, in some cases, doing ourselves more harm than good.

Given that we ate in a fairly balanced way for years without knowing much about it, you don't need to become a dietary expert to know what kinds of food to eat for good nutrition. When I was writing this book, this was the most difficult chapter. There are literally hundreds of books and thousands of studies for us to refer to when exploring what we should or shouldn't eat to maintain good or optimal health. Unfortunately, many of them overanalyze, contradict each other or are written purely for self-serving reasons, and we have been caught in the middle – dazed and confused.

The outcome has led many of us to view eating healthfully to be too complicated to execute, and the situation allows us to put up blinders to justify, excuse and deny our way out of it. So, my purpose in this chapter is to unravel the confusion and get back to the basics to give you the confidence and clear direction you need to start making better food choices.

Let me be honest by saying that I am not a nutrition expert. But as a lifelong dieter, I spent most of my life learning about every diet known to man – and subsequently failing every diet known to man. Then, after self-evaluation on the destructive nature of this practice, I discovered the "emperor has no clothes," so I've spent the last 10 years obsessed with researching and separating fact from fiction, and have come full circle with a complete faith in good old-fashioned basic science.

My final conclusion did not come from established proof in a statistic, or fancy words and explanations that seemed to make sense, but because I discovered my own balance. After years of confusion, I "cracked the code" and figured out what my body wanted and needed to maintain my weight, provide me energy and make me happy and healthy. Then I realized that what I had discovered was nothing new, but very familiar. The simple basic rules of yesterday was all I needed to know and was very easy to follow.

Therefore, the intent of this chapter is not to bombard you with scientific details or recommend an "optimum" diet for good health, but to provide an overview, or for many of you, a simple reminder of the basic science you have probably heard before but probably forgotten somewhere along the line. The information is not intended to provide you with ideals for the perfect diet, but on just achieving a balanced lifestyle and guiding principles for making better decisions.

So, don't be surprised when I don't reprimand you on the evils of eating saturated fat, go into detail on how sugar impacts your insulin levels, or scold you about shrimp being too high in cholesterol. If you are interested in learning more about nutrition, I highly encourage it. Just make sure the next book you read or website you visit educates you on the basic, tried and true fundamentals of nutrition and doesn't confuse or mislead you.

IT'S SIMPLE

If you were to learn about basic nutrition 30 years ago, the explanation would be pretty simple. Regardless of the many new theories, studies and research, there are fundamentals that cannot be denied. It's basic science – science we have known for years, even centuries.

And while there may be twists and angles for discussion, the basic foundation remains unchallenged. So, let's start there.

Food only comes in three categories: fat, protein and carbohydrates. Our bodies crave and need these foods. Carbohydrates aren't bad for you. Fat doesn't make you fat. We need all three categories of food in order for our bodies to function properly. The problem isn't the food components we eat. It's the type, quantity and the lack of balance.

Food originates from a living source – plant or animal. Animal foods contain protein and fat. Plant foods provide our carbohydrates and some plants can produce oils – such as olive, grape seed, corn or other natural plant oils. Some foods may be a combination of these, like nuts and beans that provide fat, protein and carbohydrate. If eaten in balance, these foods should provide you with your nutritional needs. If you eat a balance of protein from animals, carbohydrates from plants, and fats from animal and, preferably, plant sources, you give your body what it wants and needs to function well. As I said, I don't want to go into detail to verify why these food components are so important to a healthy diet, but I'll very briefly discuss what they are and their benefits.

Protein

Most protein sources come from the meat of animals – chicken, beef, pork, fish, ostrich, buffalo, etc. Soy is one of the few plant-based complete proteins. A lean protein is meat that does not contain much fat (the white stuff in the meat).

Your body needs protein to build and repair muscles and other body tissues, to make hormones, and to make enzymes that it needs to function normally (enzymes speed up and help certain chemical reactions to occur in your body). If you don't eat enough protein, your body may start to break down your muscle. Also, calorie for calorie, protein seems to satisfy hunger longer.

Fat

As mentioned, fat is found in both animals and plants. Dietary fat is a vital nutrient our bodies need for health and daily functioning. As an energy source, it supplies essential fatty acids for growth, healthy skin, vitamin-absorption and regulation of bodily functions.

Animal fats are saturated fats that, when consumed in excess, can clog arteries and cause heart disease and other illnesses. So, it is best to get most of your fat grams through plant sources. Most plant oils – like olive, peanut, safflower and canola oil – are monounsaturated or polyunsaturated fats and can actually improve your overall cholesterol and reduce disease. Some fish oils, like in salmon, contain Omega-3 essential fatty acids that are also very beneficial to our health.

Trans fats or hydrogenated oils – in very elementary terms – is a processed fat that seems to have the same negative affect on the body as saturated fat when excessively consumed. These fats are found in many of today's convenience foods. If I tried to go into any more detail on what a trans fat is, I would need an entire chapter – so I'll stop here.

Carbohydrates

Carbohydrates come from plant sources – fruits, vegetables, wheat, beans, oats or other grains and sugar. Carbohydrates provide us with the energy and fuel we need to function and grow, and should comprise the majority of our daily calories. Fruits and vegetables provide essential vitamins and minerals that are not provided in other food sources, and they also provide good amounts of fiber. Beans, whole wheat and other grains also provide fiber that helps us stay full longer and effectively eliminate waste. So, it is recommended that most of your carbohydrates come from these sources because they are needed to help your body function well.

While plant based, sugar doesn't provide any of these nutrients but it does provide calories, which is fuel for the body. So, foods that have essential vitamins, minerals and nutrients – foods that your body needs to function well, should be your dietary mainstay – meaning, most of your calories should come from these sources. Sugar doesn't provide any essential nutrients and although it's not necessarily bad to eat it, it doesn't provide any benefits either.

Why Fruits and Vegetables Are So Important

Because fruits and vegetables are the primary foods that provide most of our essential vitamins and minerals, it is recommended that we eat lots of them. Not only are fruits and vegetables packed with vitamins and minerals, they are loaded with thousands of compounds called phytochemicals that work together to prevent chronic diseases such as heart disease, stroke and cancer. They are also a great accompaniment to any weight loss program because they enhance feelings of fullness at a minimal caloric investment – and your body craves them.

Years ago, it was Grandma who gave us the simple rules to follow, that gave us our nutritional guidance – eat your vegetables; an apple a day keeps the doctor away; you can't have dessert until you finish your supper. If you consider that most of the foods we ate years ago came from these natural sources these rules, when followed, gave us the answer to a healthy, balanced diet.

So Why Don't We Eat Them?

The above is a pretty compelling reason to reach for a banana or a carrot. But the reality is that eighty percent of Americans do not eat the minimum recommended daily requirement of this food group. So, why don't we? Read on.

IT GOT COMPLICATED

Here is why the simple explanation got complicated. The basic science we just talked about assumes these food components are eaten in their basic form of whole, real food. With the evolution of our hectic world, we have turned to convenience foods that are mostly processed – not in their whole, natural form.

Processed foods aren't necessarily a terrible thing – they do have their place. We've processed foods for centuries. For example, churning milk into butter, making cheese or pasteurizing milk. These foods are minimally processed from their original from, but are still mostly in their whole form. Processed foods allow natural foods to be preserved so they don't go bad as quickly and can be kept for long periods of time. The problem is today's methods of turning fresh foods into processed foods changes the molecular structure of the food, robbing it of nutrients and taste. So, sugar and other nutrients are added back in to revive the taste and molecular structure.

Highly processed foods are nothing new, I remember eating Coco Puffs for breakfast in the 1960's, but we didn't rely on them as our primary food source. They were an added convenience or used as treats. So, we would consume a small amount of processed food along with our dietary mainstay of whole, unprocessed foods. Nowadays, many Americans are relying on processed foods as their primary fuel source, so they are lacking the nutrition whole foods give their bodies to stay healthy. Processed food should be an accompaniment to part of a balanced diet and should not be "in lieu of."

The Scam

Americans didn't just become defiant against proper nutrition; we have been misrepresented by the diet and food industry and have slowly allowed ourselves to fall into eating an unhealthy balance of foods. The diet and food industry has confused us into believing that foods other than whole foods are part of the dietary mainstay category. They aren't in the business of selling bananas and broccoli. As our nation became more and more concerned about health and expanding waistlines, "healthy" foods became desirable. So, responding to consumers who wanted to make healthier choices, but didn't want to give up the cookies and chips and other fun foods, the food industry strategically used healthy product labeling. As a result, we blindly concluded that we were being healthy while eating our trans fat free French fries or organic tortilla chips, our cereal with a hint of whole grain or a fruity Nutri-Grain Bar® whose first ingredient is sugar.

Food marketers can easily disguise processed foods as healthy by "fortifying" the food. Translation? They add a vitamin pill to the nutritionally void food. But don't be fooled. Nutritious food is not labeled "healthy" on a box. It's not mixed in a shake, or wrapped in hydrogenated oil and high fructose corn syrup. If a box says; light, all natural, made with whole grain, no trans fats, etc., with a few exceptions, its still junk food.

So, rather than reach for an apple instead of potato chips, we stand in the grocery aisle reading processed food labels to decide which is better for us – the one with whole grain, the low fat one, the low sodium, the one with no trans fat . . . But the reality is, when choosing a healthier breakfast option, whether it's a Pop Tart® or a Nutri-Grain Bar®, the primary ingredients are either fat or sugar. Which is worse, too much fat or too much sugar? Too much of either one isn't a good idea because it leads to too many calories and discourages you from eating the foods your body needs. Just because they sprinkle a bit of a vitamin pill in the food doesn't make the food any more nutritious.

There are some foods you might find in a grocery aisle that do provide good nutrition from fairly whole sources. For example, old-fashioned oatmeal, whole-wheat pastas, dried beans, some high protein and high fiber whole grain cereals, and a few supplement bars. By learning to read a nutrition label, you will be better able to detect the nutrition in processed foods – in all foods as well. A good website on learning to read a nutrition label is listed in the *Afterword* of this book.

The Billion Dollar Supplement Industry

To add to the damage, consumers are turning to pills, liquids and other concoctions that are supposed to replace the burden of having to eat real food by providing vitamin, mineral and fiber substitutions. Why suffer eating all that healthy stuff when you can just take this pill, juice or special vitamin water? At schools and conference rooms everywhere we are sipping what are sometimes high calorie (and expensive) special waters, alongside our burgers and fries, and blindly believing we are doing the right thing.

THERE ARE NO SUBSTITUTES FOR THE REAL THING

Americans spend 2.5 billion dollars a year on vitamins, yet cancer risks have not decreased. There is really no hard, scientific proof that taking a vitamin pill decreases the risk of cancers and other ailments. On the contrary, current research indicates there is no substitute for the real thing. Fruits and vegetables are a complex source of vitamins, minerals and phytochemicals, which all work together to prevent chronic disease. Supplements tend to work in isolation and have not proven to be as beneficial. There is also an element of risk. Taking too much of certain supplements can cause harm and need to be consumed carefully as you would any medication.

That said, there is nothing wrong with taking a daily vitamin pill, calcium, or other supplements to help round out your diet, but don't take them instead of eating nutritious food and be careful about consuming them in excess.

SO WHAT ARE YOU EATING?

If you are taking supplements as an alternative to eating the real thing, then what are you eating? When you consider that two-thirds of Americans are overweight or obese, 80 percent do not get the minimum number of fruits and vegetables, and even fewer achieve the minimum daily fiber requirement, suffice it to say that the American diet is mostly fat and sugar. Therefore, the real eye opener for you might not be that you aren't getting enough whole food nutrients and fiber, it's realizing what foods you are eating instead!

A SIMPLE COMMITMENT

So when asking yourself, "What foods should I eat?", make these simple commitments to yourself throughout your day, and you will be on your way to a nutritionally balanced diet:

♦ Eat more whole foods – especially fruits and vegetables (found in the produce aisle – not in a gummy snack).

♦ Consider processed foods more of a treat to enjoy only after you've eaten the foods your body needs to be healthy.

If your diet is not rich in fruits and vegetables now, don't worry about what types are best for you, just eat them. Better yet, eat a variety of them. The more varied the foods the better, because the phytochemicals, vitamins and minerals work together to promote overall health. Generally, the brighter the color of the vegetables, the more nutritious, so it is best to include them daily for optimal benefit.

As your dietary mainstay, include the other excellent natural sources of foods to round out your balanced diet – lean protein, legumes and nuts, whole grains, and dairy. As a general rule, if it comes directly from a plant or animal source with minimal processing, it's whole food.

STOP THE EXCUSES

As we discussed earlier, if you rely on excuses you will most likely not be successful. Eighty percent of Americans do not get the minimum recommendation of five servings a day of fruits and vegetables. When asked why they don't, their excuses are rarely because they don't like these foods. Rather, the answer will typically be that fruits and vegetables are inconvenient, expensive or go bad before they have a chance to eat them. Let's talk about this, so we can eliminate these excuses that are holding you back from making better decisions.

They are inconvenient

Fruit and vegetables are as readily available as chips, cookies, donuts or other sugary carbohydrates. You can grab a banana, apple or bag of baby carrots at any grocery store and most convenience marts. Many stores are pre-packaging fruit salads, celery and peanut butter and other healthier items, and you can always bring them from home with just a minute of preparation.

Cooking with vegetables is as easy as any convenience food. You can steam fresh vegetables in about five minutes with a swish of a pan for cleanup. Frozen vegetables can be microwaved in their own bag.

Most restaurants offer vegetables as a side if you ask, and you can also ask for them as a substitute for French fries. Admittedly, fast food restaurants suffer from lack of choices, but you can snack on nutritious food to make up for the lack of vegetables at your meal.

The reality is that healthy foods are not inconvenient, we just choose not to think about our options and use excuses instead.

They are expensive

The price of nine servings of bananas is about $1.89 depending on the time of year and where you live. The price of a nine-serving bag of Doritos is $2.69. With the banana you get vitamins, minerals and fiber. With the Doritos you get pretty much nothing in the way of nutritional value. Oh, but it tastes so good! Regardless, you get more VALUE from the banana. The reason fruits and vegetables become more expensive is that we buy the bananas and the Doritos, eat the Doritos, throw the bananas away, and later claim the bananas are just too expensive to buy again.

But, of course, prices do vary and often it depends on the season. So, buy whatever is on sale, looks good and you like.

They go bad

Then eat them! Just as in the example above, the produce you buy goes bad because you choose to eat other, less healthy foods instead. We go to the store in our "I'm going to be healthy" mood, and then let the healthy food rot in the fridge while we stress out on a pizza.

Here are some ways to incorporate fruits and vegetables into your otherwise not so perfect diet:

- There isn't a rule that says you can only have vegetables if you are having a healthy meal. We think everything has to be unhealthy or healthy – there is room for us all to get along. So steam up some broccoli with your hot dog!

- Always keep raw vegetables around. If you don't get fruits and vegetables with your meals, snack on them throughout the day. Frozen fruits and vegetables are affordable, always available and as nutritious, if not more, than fresh.

- Nosh on them while you are cooking dinner. As I mentioned earlier, if you pick on some raw veggies instead of chips or bread, you will have staved off hunger, not spoiled your dinner, and received a huge amount of nutrition.

- You can also snack on dried fruit in moderation and use frozen fruits for treats - great for smoothies

- Add more vegetables to soups, omelets, pastas and other dishes.

People who have a balanced diet will tell you that fitting healthier foods into their diet is not difficult. They simply made a decision to do it.

Balance Your Diet

To maintain a generally balanced diet, follow these simple rules:

♦ Whole foods should be your dietary mainstay — fruits, vegetables, lean protein, whole grains, dairy, nuts and legumes.

♦ Enjoy processed foods and treats in moderation.

♦ Fruits and vegetables provide the essential vitamins and minerals to keep your body functioning well — so eat as much as you can every day. As your grandma would say: "Eat your vegetables. They're good for you." or "An apple a day keeps the doctor away!"

♦ It is OK to eat some foods that do not contain the nutrition your body needs, but they shouldn't be your primary source of food. As your grandma would say: "You can't have dessert until you finish your supper."

♦ If you aren't eating food that is naturally nutritious, you are most likely eating the majority of your calories in the form of fat and sugar — usually providing more calories than your body needs, and resulting in weight gain and poor health.

9

The Realities of Weight Loss

Adding good nutrition to your diet is the best way to keep your body functioning well and it can also be a benefit to weight loss, but a healthier diet does not necessarily mean you will lose weight. There has been much confusion over this distinction in recent years. Obesity rates have skyrocketed in this country and at the same time there have been hundreds of diet theories that have taken new approaches– usually called by the proponent as an "easy" approach – to losing weight. Most of these diets focus on the types of food you eat and, while that focus is important, they have caused much of the confusion. In this chapter, we are going to return to the fundamentals of weight loss – basic science that we know is true and has been tested and proven throughout time.

UNDERSTANDING THE BASIC CONCEPT OF WEIGHT LOSS

The conflict of theories has us confused as to what to consider when trying to lose weight. We look at a label and question, "Should I worry about the fat, the fiber, the sugar or the calories?" With each new theory, there is a different angle, including how often you eat and in what combination you should eat the recommended foods.

Media sound bites, articles and resources try to give us tidbits of useful information to help us along. Unfortunately, the positive or negative findings in these reports depends on what point they are trying to make. For example, an article might say that chicken vegetable soup is a great choice for health and weight loss because it is full of vegetables and low in calories. Another report may say that it's a bad choice because soup is high in sodium. Yet another may claim that a fast food joint's whole grain sandwich may be healthier for you than a hamburger. And, while containing more fiber, the healthier sandwich may also have several hundred more calories and twice as much sodium as the hamburger.

CALORIES IN - CALORIES OUT

While it is certainly important to consider fiber, vitamins and minerals, fat and sugar, if you are trying to find the answer to weight loss, your primary focus should be on the calories. Regardless of the diet theory, the reason you lose weight is either because you have taken in fewer calories than your body needs over time, or you've expended more calories through exercise – ideally, a combination of both. As natural bodybuilder Tom Venuto states quite well, "*The law of calorie balance is an unbreakable law of physics – energy in versus energy out dictates whether you will gain, lose or maintain your weight. Period.*"

As I mentioned before, food only comes in three categories – fat, protein and carbohydrate – that are all measured in calories. So, counting anything other than calories, as a primary consideration, is just more complicated and restrictive. The advantage to getting educated on calories is that you can eat any kind of food and still lose weight. You could theoretically go on the M&M diet. Eat nothing but M&M's everyday and you will lose weight. Why? For two reasons:

1. As long as you eat fewer calories than your body needs you will lose weight – even if those calories are provided just by M&M's.

2. You will get tired of eating M&M's and will crave something else, therefore, no matter how much you like M&M's, you will eat fewer M&M's as days go by.

Now, of course a diet of M&M's is not condoned, but in theory, it would work. The point is that losing weight by controlling calories is the easiest way to lose weight because you don't have to give up the foods you love. Diet programs such as Weight Watchers, Jenny Craig, and Nutri-system use calories as the "magic" in their program. Whether it's a point or a portion – they are measuring calories.

Diet programs became popular because we don't have to go to the trouble of counting calories in order to lose a few pounds. We want a simple, "magic" way to lose weight – only there isn't any. Many so-called "easy ways" to weight loss require you to give up foods you love or require special meals that don't fit into your life, and then it becomes too complicated to execute and is a sacrifice. Now that it's come full circle in today's world, counting calories has become the "easy way." Maintaining your weight with an eye on calories allows you to be in control – to choose what foods you need to keep you balanced, how much your body needs, and fit them nicely into your balanced lifestyle.

So, let's talk about how many calories your body needs and the amounts that are in the foods you eat so you can design your plan to maintain or lose weight.

How Many Calories Are Too Many Calories?

The amount of calories a person needs varies and is generally based on age, sex, height and activity level. Metabolism does factor into it to a certain extent, as does taking certain medications. On average, a 40-year-old woman who is moderately active needs about 1800-2000 calories a day to maintain her weight; a 40-year-old man, about 2250-2500 calories per day. To get a more accurate estimate on your caloric needs, I suggest you go to www.mypyramid.gov and click "My Pyramid Plan." Do their online calculation. It's simple and fun.

The Grim Reality

Unfortunately, due to our excessive food environment, we have lost touch with how much food our bodies actually need and our daily consumption of food is on a weight-gaining pattern. Our average day's calories are more than our body needs, so even though we may follow a diet on some days, overall, we are still taking in more calories than our bodies need and aren't making any headway to actual long-term weight loss.

HOW FAST CAN YOU REALISTICALLY LOSE WEIGHT?

If you take in or expend fewer calories than your body needs, and you do it consistently over a period of time, you will lose weight. Now here is the reality: on average, you need a deficit of 3500 calories to lose a pound. Transversely, if you eat 3500 calories more than your body needs you will gain a pound. To lose a pound a week, you would have to consistently net out 500 fewer calories per day (500 X 7 = 3500) than your body needs. If you have 20 pounds to lose, you can expect to lose about 1–2 pounds per week if you are consistent with your efforts. You should expect to lose 20 pounds in about four to six months.

The more you have to lose, the faster you can lose it. When you hear about the person who lost 100 pounds in six months it sounds unbelievable. Actually, it's a lot easier to lose 100 pounds than the final 10 pounds. Why, you ask? Because if you are 100 pounds over-weight, you are most likely eating a lot of food – let's say on average 3500 calories a day. If you just stopped overeating you would eat 1500 fewer calories per day, thus losing approximately three pounds a week without much of an effort. Add to that an exercise program, and one could actually lose 100 pounds in six months.

Why is it so hard to lose the last 10 pounds? Many people have those last stubborn 10 pounds that they try and try to lose without success. Here's why. If you are only 10 pounds overweight, you prob-ably are not overeating too much. Maybe a few hundred calories here or there, which when added up over a long period of time, slowly impact the scale.

If you want to lose those pounds, you have to be very diligent and patient. Since you aren't eating an excessive amount of calories, you can only reduce them a little or your body will not have enough calories to sustain good metabolic function. Losing weight becomes a balancing act. If you have a strong desire to be the perfect weight, that's great. Just be prepared to be dedicated over a long period of time. Otherwise, accept the 10 pounds and focus on staying active, eating the right foods and not adding another 10.

BUDGETING CALORIES

Counting calories is the easiest way to weight loss, but it does require a little investigative work. Years ago, calorie counting wasn't so easy. But with product labeling and the convenience of the Internet, finding out how many calories are in the foods you eat can be fun. If you know approximately how many calories you want to consume a day, counting calories is like being on a budget. How many calories do you have a day and how are you going to use them? If you think about it, you probably eat pretty much the same food items over a period of time out of habit. Find out how many calories are in those foods and then you can design your own food plan – considering the amount of calories you have to spend, your nutritional needs (kind of like the rent, electricity), and what calories you have left over for entertainment. If you eat too many calories at a meal and end up going over your budget, simply pay back the loan by eating fewer calories or healthier foods until the loan is paid back.

As you learn how many calories are in the foods you eat, you can eventually make knowledgeable food selections without even looking them up. As I mentioned, in the *Afterword* of this book, I provide a few websites that will help you decipher a nutrition label, calorie and other information on restaurant choices and other foods as well. While this may sound grueling, if you really want to change your behaviors, you will find it interesting and empowering.

My clients find it a real eye-opener when they realize just how damaging some of their food choices have been. And as a result, they happily rid themselves of the culprit. They become better consumers of food, finding a real interest in educating themselves and making better decisions.

CONSISTENCY IS KEY

You have to look at weight loss over a span of time. It's not about how much you eat or don't eat in one day. It's cumulative over a long period of time. For example, when trying to lose weight, you may have a few good days when you are mindful of your calories and are on your way to weight loss success, but then you mindlessly indulge in an 800-calorie, stress related Cinnabon fix – your reward for being good the few days before. The end result is you are right back where you started. We then presume that our diet isn't working, or our metabolism is slow – we've tried, but we just can't lose weight. We don't recognize just how damaging these slips can be. We think that as long as we were good on some days, we should still lose weight. Unfortunately, it's not that easy. While you can indulge, you need to recognize the impact the indulgence is having on your effort. Instead of thinking, "Oh, it was just one Cinnabon." If you know the Cinnabon is 800 calories (nearly half a day's worth of calories for weight maintenance) then you can make a more educated decision. Accept the reality of its potential damage and consider whether it's worth spending.

One Bad Day Can Ruin a Whole Week's Effort

Another example of consistency is the notion that if we're good all week, we can splurge on the weekends and still lose weight. And, while you can loosen up on the weekends or other times and still lose weight, you have to make sure you indulge moderately so you don't negate your good decisions made earlier in the week. It's one thing to have a dessert or a few glasses of wine, but if you gorge excessively you will ruin your week's efforts. Some people are capable of consuming a thousand calories or more than their body needs at any one meal if they allow themselves. If you are guilty of this, recognize that your weight loss efforts need to address the gorging behavior first. You can let your guard down, but you must still be mindful of your actions to be successful.

DESIGNING YOUR OWN MODERATION AND BALANCE WEIGHT LOSS PLAN

In designing your own plan, consider what foods are most important to you and what foods you can live without. Rather than give them up, incorporate them into your weight loss and balanced eating plan. If you can't live without something, then what can you trade up that isn't as important to you? For example:

You can't end the day without a chocolate fix:

Instead of giving up your treat or relying on a not so tasty substitute, buy some really good chocolate (I recommend Ghirardelli dark chocolate squares) and keep them on hand for a daily chocolate fix. One Ghirardelli chocolate square is 70 calories, half the calories of a Nutrigrain bar – so you can have two of them (140 calories) for the same calories and much more pleasure. Eat them slowly and enjoy the moment.

If you are a daily dessert lover, decide how you will work in those fun calories into your overall balanced diet. For example, add extra vegetables at dinner and forego the rice or bread or take a 20-minute walk after dinner.

You love potato chips and other salty snacks:

Let's say your typical lunch is a sandwich with potato chips. Instead of giving up the potato chips, use only one slice of bread, a half a slice of cheese and add some carrots on the side. You end up with about the same amount of calories and better overall nutrition. (Just keep an eye on how many chips you eat!)

You love cheese:

Cheese is mostly fat and the calories add up. If you really love cheese, simply either ask for less cheese or pull some of the cheese off of the food yourself – remember the Taste Adaptation we talked about? When choosing cheese, consider cheese that is dense in flavor like Feta, Goat, Asiago or Romano. Processed cheeses like American have very little flavor, and people become adapted to the texture rather than the taste.

A SNAPSHOT OF MODERATION AND BALANCED EATING

If this were a typical diet book, I would provide you with sample eating plans or tell you what foods you should or shouldn't have. With moderation and balance eating, you make the decision. So, let's talk about how to put a balanced eating plan together. Below is a general breakdown of your daily caloric needs based on the principles of moderation and balance eating. You can fill in the foods that go into your meals, being mindful of the balanced nutrition we discussed in Chapter 8.

DAILY CALORIE NEEDS	
40 year-old woman, moderately active, weighs 145 pounds	
TARGET FOR WEIGHT MAINTENANCE	
Calories	**1800-2000**
Daily Breakdown	
Per meal (3 meals)	400–600
Snacks for day	200–500

The chart gives you a range of calories to spread throughout the day based on the approximate number allowed for weight maintenance. These numbers are just an example and will vary depending on your age, sex and activity level. When designing your plan consider the following:

♦ Balance your calories throughout your day by eating three moderate meals and snacks to keep your metabolism running well

♦ Include ample amounts of vegetables, fruits and whole grains, and a serving of protein at each meal

♦ Processed and fun foods can be enjoyed in moderation once nutritional needs are met and overall calories stay within range

♦ If you overindulge on occasion, simply minimize snacks or reduce calories in your next meal to "pay back" the loan

The range gives you flexibility in your caloric intake to accommodate what comes your way in life. For example, if on Friday night you have two pieces of pizza and a beer and exceed your 600-calorie meal maximum, you simply eat lower calorie meals or reduce snack calories until you've "paid back" the excess calories. But as I cautioned earlier, you still need to keep your meal indulgences in moderation – for example, maybe 800–900 calories – not 1200-1500 calories. This amount of excess, if it were to happen a few times a week, would be difficult to make up and would result in weight gain.

For Weight Loss

The above provides an example to "maintain" your weight. To lose weight, reduce the amount of calories for weight maintenance by about 20 percent - for a 2000 calorie a day diet, about 400 calories. Or, ideally, reduce calories by less than 20 percent but increase your physical activity. Or both. So, this will take some effort, but if you are consistent and patient, instead of trying to lose weight in an unrealistic amount of time, you will succeed. Once you've succeeded, you can enjoy your targeted calorie allowance for weight maintenance, instead of yo-yoing back and forth from sacrifice and deprivation, to over-indulgence and binging.

WEIGHT LOSS MADE SIMPLE

If my explanation of the moderation and balance example has your head spinning and you have concluded it's too much thinking for right now, just try this simple example of a successful weight loss plan:

> *I ran into an old friend I hadn't seen in a year, and he had dropped about 50 pounds. He looked great! I asked him, "How did you do it!" He said, "You know, I tried all those diets and none of them worked for me. Here's what I did. I ate everything I always did, but I ate half and I couldn't believe how fast I lost weight!"*

It's amazing how the diet world has caused us to be so misinformed that one considers it a revelation that if you eat less, you'll weigh less. So, if you are not up to spending the time analyzing the calories in the foods you eat, start off by simply eating less than you do now. That's it! If you consistently eat less of the same foods you eat now, you will lose weight. If you add more fruits and vegetables to your diet and move your body a little more, you will be on your way to a healthy, balanced lifestyle. The formula works easily if done consistently.

The Realities of Weight Loss

For weight loss, follow these guidelines

- Calories are the most important factor of weight loss or gain
- Determine how many calories you need a day (www. mypyramid.gov)
- Learn how many calories are in the foods you routinely eat
- Include good nutrition in your calories to help keep your body satisfied
- Be consistent in your efforts – one day of overindulgence can ruin your efforts
- Budget your calories and pay back "loans" of excessive calories to maintain your weight
- By overcoming your mental obstacles to change and listening to your body, a moderation and balance diet will become natural to you and weight loss can be maintained forever

10

Myths, Misinformation and Other Stuff that Keep Us from Success

*B*ecause most Americans are confused about what to eat and how we gain or lose weight, we buy into the sound bites we hear, which results in poor choices and contributes to the ill health and obesity problem in this country. When considering our food choices, we don't rely on the basics as I explained previously (i.e., real food is nutritious food and calories in, calories out). Instead, we buy into biased information and new theories that contradict basic science and make it even more difficult to make good decisions. We may think we are making better decisions when we're not even close. Here are a few widely known theories, plus an explanation of why they have caused more harm than good in solving our nation's unhealthy lifestyle problem:

"CARBOHYDRATES ARE BAD FOR YOU"

Carbohydrates are the body's primary fuel source. Muscles prefer them and the brain relies on them. In fact, carbohydrates are so crucial to the body, that if you severely cut them from your diet, your body will begin to break down muscle and other protein-containing tissues – your heart and other vital organs – in order to make them.

If a food isn't a fat or protein, it's a carbohydrate – so by restricting carbohydrates from your diet, you are omitting most of your food options as well – some of them excellent sources of nutrition. Some popular theories and diets have indicated that some fruits and/or vegetables and other whole food carbohydrates cause weight gain or sugar spikes and should not be consumed. To consider that any fruit or vegetable is unhealthy for you and should not be eaten is ridiculous. The potato, for example, has received a lot of negative publicity. When, in fact, the potato is probably one of the best foods you can eat. An average potato has almost 50 percent of daily vitamin C, as much potassium as spinach, has no fat and is 100 calories. The skin is also an excellent source of fiber. The problem isn't the potato, it's what we torture the potato with – oil, cheese, sour cream, butter and bacon!

Diets that restrict certain whole foods from our diets are just an absurd twist to reducing the amount of calories in your diet – remember, the calorie is the indicator of weight loss or gain. Some carbohydrates like lettuce, broccoli, and peppers are very low in calories while others like whole grains, beans and potatoes are higher in calories. As I explained before, healthy food does not translate to weight loss; reduction in calories does. But, restricting calories by eliminating healthy "real" food from your diet is not a productive way to lose weight and maintain good health.

If the carbohydrate is from a whole, natural food, then it's good for you and should be included in your weight loss or maintenance plan. However, you still need to keep an eye on your overall daily calorie intake to maintain or lose weight – moderation along with your balance.

"FATS MAKE YOU FAT"

No, but too much does, and we Americans are drowning in it. Too much saturated or trans fats are a problem because they can block arteries and increase cholesterol. But as I briefly discussed before, plant fats can actually improve arteries and reduce cholesterol. Regardless of what kind of fat, it's important to moderate your intake for weight loss or maintenance. Whether the fats come from heart healthy olive oil, or artery clogging butter, they still have the same amount of calories and are the leading cause of weight gain – more than any other food – for two reasons:

1. Fat has more calories per gram – nine calories per gram versus carbs and protein, which each only have four. Therefore, it is denser.

2. Fat is easily hidden in the foods we eat, especially restaurant and convenience foods.

Let me explain. Since fat has more calories per gram, it's easier to consume more calories than your body needs and that causes weight gain. Think about it. A serving of lean protein, say a boneless chicken breast, has about 140 or so calories and is the size of a deck of cards. The same size portion of fat is about 800 calories. Wow!

Now, think how easy it is to add extra fat (calories) to any dish. It is not only denser, but it is a liquid or it can melt, so it can take up very little room on your plate. You can easily transform a 400-calorie pasta dish into 1200 calories without visually noticing the difference. Most restaurants and fast food joints have a policy of "the cheesier, fried or buttery the better," and they serve the fare in ridiculously huge portions. This is a combustible combination that's exploding our country's waistlines and poor health. We are eating loads of unhealthy calories without even recognizing it. All this has contributed to the American's standard diet preference for fatty foods and has accustomed us to regularly eating too many calories.

THE LOW FAT VERSUS LOW CARB WARS

Over the last decade or so, there has been a war of sorts over the low fat versus low carbohydrate dietary recommendations. Various studies have proclaimed either side the victor, but in every study, there is always some variance or some missing factor that skews the findings. One study might show how much weight was lost the fastest, but not how much weight was lost the longest. Or, how much scale weight was lost, versus how much fat loss. Or some other non-equitable analysis. Does it really matter? Bottom line is, whether it's a fat or carbohydrate, weight loss or gain is still determined by how many calories you take in or expend, and food from whole food sources has better nutrition than processed food. So, how did this controversial war come about?

Low fat diets started it. About 20 years or so ago, there was an increase in heart disease and obesity in our country, and dietary experts pointed to the increase in excessive fat consumption in the American diet as a leading culprit. (Correctly so, I might add.) The recommendation was simple. Eat a balanced diet but reduce the amount of high fat foods. Take in fewer calories and, therefore, lose weight. And, if you reduce the amount of saturated (bad) fat in your diet, you reduce the risk of heart disease.

But then came the diet bandwagon. The diet and food industry, as well as Americans, went low fat crazy and took the reasonable, healthy recommendation out of balance. Instead of eating a balanced diet lower in fat, and increasing consumption of real sources like fruits, vegetables and whole grains, Americans started to pig out on anything that was low fat regardless of its nutritional or caloric value. Food marketers capitalized on the movement by developing and selling processed junk food – as long as it was low fat, it was deemed to be healthy for you. Then hundreds of diet books with their twist on theories of how to eat low fat foods were hitting the best-seller lists, and the American public started eating anything that was low fat as being good for you regardless of how many calories it had.

Cookies, chips, candy and other beloved foods were given a low fat makeover and the foods went flying off the shelves. We munched all day on pretzels, jellybeans, licorice, rice cakes and fat-free Fig Newtons, blindly thinking we were making the right choices.

We started replacing our love of fat with a love of sugar. The reality was the low fat versions may have had lower fat, but the fat was replaced with sugar. Overall, the caloric value went down very little so we were still eating too many calories and little nutrition.

I bought into it too. I can remember we had this wonderful bread bakery nearby, where I would buy a warm loaf and eat three or so slices while driving home – guilt free. Then I find out later and wiser that each slice was 150 calories. So, I sat and ate the calorie equivalent of two donuts while being "good." To top it off, I wasn't really satisfied with those calories because it was nothing but processed white flour with very little nutritional value.

So, instead of too much fat, Americans started eating too much sugar – and instead of losing weight, we kept gaining. Then we became so called "sugar addicts" and instead of lowering cholesterol, the marketed diet encouraged the spread of Type II diabetes.

The low fat diet set the stage for hundreds of other diet theories to follow – none of them as reasonable or effective as simple moderation and balance.

The good news is that it seems there is a ray of hope that the diet wars may be winding down and that we may live peacefully again, where Americans can be healthy and still enjoy their favorite foods!

MINI-MEALS VERSUS THREE-SQUARE MEALS THEORY

Lately, we hear experts dismiss the standard three square meals a day lifestyle in favor of the mini-meal concept. The gurus say by eating five or six small meals a day, every few hours, your metabolism will be stoked and you will burn more calories. The problem is that it is unrealistic for many people to have access to food that frequently and you never really get to have a nice, satisfying meal. The reality is the mini-meal theory is pretty much the typical three-square meal, moderation and balance eating, only repackaged to be more inconvenient and complicated to follow.

Here's the simple deal: If you do not overeat at any one meal and eat a balance of foods, you should be hungry approximately every four hours. Okay, so 8:00 am breakfast, 12:00 noon lunch, and dinner used to be between 5:00 and 6:00 pm. To stave off hunger during the lunch-dinner time, we had what was called a snack to tie us over due to the longer duration between meals. Then, we also had what was known as dessert after dinner (but only if you finished your plate and ate your vegetables!). So, to me, that's eating five times a day.

Now here is where we get into trouble. We don't eat at 5:00 pm any more. Instead, many of us eat between 7:00 and 9:00 pm. So, what happens? If you don't have a light snack to tie you over, you are starving and then gorge yourself on dinner. Or, our "light" snack is nearly a meal's worth of calories, and so we end up eating the calorie equivalent of two meals.

We don't need to eat mini-meals, we simply need to eat three balanced meals with light snacks in between if we are hungry. What's really going on with the American diet is we are overeating at meals, or skipping meals, and we are not eating in moderation, nor are we balancing our calories throughout the day. By going hungry or overstuffing ourselves, our metabolism can become out of balance and in the end, we simply end up eating too many calories.

So, rather than follow a theory that is difficult to practice in real life, simply eat moderately balanced three square meals a day (breakfast, lunch and dinner) like we used to before we were so out of balance. If you haven't overeaten at your meals you will probably want a light snack or two daily. If you adapt to eating when you are hungry and stopping when you are full, you don't have to adhere to any method of eating.

MAKING CHOICES

As we wade our way through a sea of fast food, chain restaurants and convenience stores, we make attempts to do the right thing by choosing items that we believe are healthier for us. In many cases, we are being led down a path of misinformed choices. There was a recent book published by *Men's Health* magazine called *Eat This, Not That*, which revealed some of these misconceptions. The book was designed to help readers make better choices at popular restaurants. While it doesn't go far enough to educate consumers, it does make the point that people need to be better informed about their choices when eating out and offers some suggestions on how to do so. Here are a few common culprits that keep us from making informed choices:

The Scary Salad

When perusing a restaurant menu, many dieters decide on salads as a better choice to control their weight and end up getting much more (calories) than they bargained for. Years ago a salad was on a plate half the size of a dinner plate, consisting mostly of fresh vegetables and dressing.

Today, the salads are in a huge bowl and may contain meats (sometimes fried), cheese, egg, bacon, nuts, tortilla strips or wonton noodles, along with a half a cup of salad dressing to accompany such a large portion. Some salads are more calories than the burgers on the menu. Consider that a restaurant cheeseburger is typically around 850 calories (which is a lot) and compare that to the popular salads below:

Ruby Tuesday Carolina Chicken	870 calories
Applebee's Grilled Steak Caesar	1200 calories
Chili's Southwestern Cob	970 calories

SUGGESTION: Instead of a salad, choose a grilled protein sandwich without cheese and ask for steamed vegetables instead of fries. Calories saved: about 400–500.   .

Deceptive Descriptions

While we can all accept that the Fettuccine Alfredo at Olive Garden may be worth a day's calories, many of us get lured into menu items that sound healthy, but are outrageously high in calories and fat. Consider a few of these:

Ruby Tuesday Grilled Chicken Broccoli Pasta (*without sides*)	1680 calories
Ruby Tuesday Bella Ground Turkey Burger (*without sides*)	1140 calories

The Big Mac Attacked

The Big Mac has always gotten a bad rap (as it should) but is its evil reputation as deserved as we claim? I don't think so. Not when you compare it to other sandwiches we buy into that we think are better choices, for example:

Specialty delis like Panera Bread are marketed and perceived to offer healthier choices than traditional fast food restaurants. But as we flock to make the better choices at a higher price, we are being led down a fat and calorie laden path. Most Panera Bread specialty sandwiches are between 700 and 850 calories and loaded with fat and sodium. Compare them to a Big Mac with only 540 calories, less fat and sometimes far less sodium. Yet, we are blissfully lunching at these restaurants feeling good about our choices.

Subway spent millions attacking the Big Mac, comparing it to their healthier low fat sandwich. However, when you look at the fine print, the Subway sandwich they are comparing says the sandwich contains no cheese or oil. Well, if you took the sauce and cheese off the Big Mac, the comparison would change dramatically. And, what's more, once you move off the advertised healthy sub list, most of Subway's sandwiches can be very high in calories – just as high, if not more, than any McDonald's sandwich on their menu. As a result of this deceptive advertising, many people head to Subway and buy a meatball sub and justify it by assuming they are making a healthier choice.

The Big Mac debuted in 1968 and it was a BIG sandwich. But in today's super-size world, the Big Mac is now the not-so-Big Mac. Still a big sandwich, but there are a lot bigger competitors out there. Of course, the point is not to suggest we start eating Big Macs, but that it's unfortunate that our efforts to do the right thing are not leading us to better health or weight loss.

Fast Food, or Not-So-Fast Food

Drive-thru lines can be tediously long. If you are at a drive-thru at prime time, the line can wrap around the restaurant and, sometimes, out into the street. When I ask people how long it takes to do drive-thru from the time you enter the parking lot to exit during busy hours, the answer is typically 15 minutes. In 15 minutes, I can make you a salmon filet with capers, onion and lemon, accompanied by vegetables and a quick one-pan cleanup.

RESTAURANT TIPS

Eating out at restaurants does provide challenges, but typically there are at least a few healthier choices available. Regardless of how much they serve you, you still have control as to how much you eat and do not be afraid to demand healthier versions of their not so healthy entrees. Here are some tips that can help you enjoy eating out without overdoing it:

- Split an entrée and/or ask for a doggy bag with the meal
- Eat an appetizer instead of a main course
- Ask for your food to be prepared with less oil, cheese or butter
- Ask for dressing on the side
- Have the waiter take your plate as soon as you're full
- Have the waiter bring a take-home container with your meal
- Bypass the bread or chips
- Order more veggies
- Have a kids meal

And a recommendation from a reformed restaurant binger – shake salt all over your food when your stomach says it's full!

THE BEST ADVICE TO AVOID RESTAURANT TRAPS — EAT AT HOME!

Eating at home can be cheaper, easier, less stressful and tastier – once you make the decision to do it. Most of our resistance to preparing food from home comes from the blinders we have – we just don't want to think about it. But, if you do, you will find that it's not that difficult. It's easier to eat a bowl of cereal at home than run into Starbucks or McDonalds. Packing a brown bag lunch takes a simple minute or two versus wasting your valuable lunchtime sitting at a drive-thru. Preparing simple meals at home in your comfy sweats, as opposed to sitting in a loud restaurant with bad service, makes for a much more relaxing evening. And there is nothing wrong with whipping up omelets, a bowl of soup or a grilled tomato and cheese sandwich in a pinch. Supermarkets provide so many short-cuts to help us out. The advantage is that you are in control of what is prepared and you don't get caught up in the excesses. And, if you make a consistent effort to eat more from home, you can go on vacation to an island 20 pounds thinner with the money and calories you've saved!

Some tips for eating at home:

◆ Keep cut-up fruits and vegetables and already-cooked lean protein in the fridge

◆ Cook with less cheese and fat, replacing them with broth or wine

◆ Use dense, flavorful cheeses like Feta, Goat or Asiago – a little goes a long way on flavor

◆ Eat breakfast at home, or bring it to work

◆ Keep protein thawing in the fridge

◆ Choose serving size cuts of protein that cook and thaw quickly

♦ Always have frozen vegetables and fruit on hand

♦ Always serve vegetables with your meal

♦ Use smaller plates

♦ Pack your lunch

♦ Keep an eye on the serving size

♦ Don't drink your calories

♦ Serve meals from the stove – so you have to get up for seconds

Be a Better Consumer of Food

I know I've given you a lot of information to digest, but I thought it was important that you be aware of the misleading information you may have been absorbing all around you. By being aware of deceptions and food traps and debunking myths you will be more educated and less confused. Summarizing what we've learned:

♦ Most diet theories are simply unconstructive and confusing spins on the basic principles of science – calories in-calories out.

♦ Become a better "consumer" of food by learning the real truth behind restaurant choices and not buying into misleading marketing.

♦ The best way to be a better "consumer" of food is to eat at home.

♦ Moderation and balance is the easiest way to apply good nutrition, weight loss or maintenance, in our hectic out of balance world.

11

Just Get Up and Do Something!

*N*ow that we've educated you on calories in, let's start tackling calories out through expending more energy.

We're always talking about the importance of exercise these days. How long should we exercise, at what intensity, what equipment to use. Yet, the biggest obstacle still remains that we just don't do it! We buy the equipment, join the gym, get the great yoga outfit, buy the expensive bike. We've got all the tapes, toys, products and gadgets to get us fit in a jiffy. And it seems the ones who buy the most, use them the least. We are looking for something to make it happen for us – to motivate us from the outside, when the motivation lies within each of us.

My goal is to get you motivated to take the initial steps to just do something more than you are doing now, do it consistently and make it a habit. Once it's a habit and a part of your daily life, you can push yourself to do more. It will be easier because it will be something you want to do, not have to do. You will have the basic foundation laid to help you reach your unlimited potential.

THE DREADED "E" WORD

When you say the word "exercise" many people go: "Ugh! I hate to exercise!" or "I would love to exercise, but who has the time!" So, my first priority is to get you to overcome your resistance and excuses surrounding that dirty word by trying to motivate you to be physically active instead. Let's take a look at the definition.

Exercise – Physical activity that is a planned, structured movement of the body designed to reach a goal of enhanced physical fitness

Activity – Energetic action or movement; liveliness

While you might dread exercise, how can you say you don't want to be – or don't have time to be – lively and energetic? So, how about from this point forward, I help motivate you to become more lively and energetic, instead of planning, structuring and being goal-oriented through exercise? If you can at least be more physically active, you are on your way to better health, weight loss and a more balanced life.

OUR ENVIRONMENTAL REALITY

For most of us, it's not that we don't get regular exercise; we simply aren't moving! In our current environment, moving our bodies has become optional. Many of us only move to get from point A to point B, and the distance keeps getting shorter and shorter. We get up, walk to the shower, walk out the door, walk to our desk, walk to the bathroom, walk to get coffee (and a donut), walk to our car, and then walk back in the house. Meanwhile, during the other 16 hours of our day, many of us are on our butts. This is not normal. To conquer this, we advocate exercise to offset our sedentary lifestyle. But because it has such a grueling appeal to many of us, we avoid it, make excuses and resist it.

Years ago, few of us exercised. We didn't belong to gyms, own treadmills, go to classes, or have a collection of exercise DVD's. Yet we were physically active. We walked the golf course, hung clothes on the line, mowed our lawns with a manual lawn mower, scrubbed our floors on our hands and knees, and didn't have computers or 150-channel remote controlled cable. Our bodies were used to moving and we weren't resistant to it. I remember my parents, even in their fifties and beyond, would go on nature walks, went sledding on the hill when it snowed, and danced at their parties. They also played tennis. They didn't belong to the Club or invest in equipment. They had the same racquets for 20 years and they went to the high school courts to play. They weren't very good at the game, but it didn't matter. They were spending time together on a beautiful Saturday afternoon. Today, spending time together would most likely mean watching movies or a trip to the mall and a stop at Chili's.

INACTIVITY TAKES A DOWNWARD SPIRAL

The more sedentary you are, the more resistant you become to moving your body. We've all had that feeling when you are contently moving around "doing" things like the dishes, laundry, taking out the trash and you aren't even thinking about the fact that you are engaged in physical activity. Then you sit down on the couch to watch a TV show and you are reluctant to get up and move again to go to bed, let alone get up to exercise!

Over a period of time, if you continue to live in a state where you are simply moving only when you have to for your daily needs, your body starts to break down, your joint and muscle ability starts to decline. Your heart may be affected, and you face the possibility of becoming disabled. It can definitely shorten your life.

EXERCISE: AN EFFECTIVE RX

Our bodies need regular exercise in order to be healthy, and getting it shouldn't be a necessity only when we want to lose weight. Lack of exercise can be more of a factor in obesity and related illnesses than our diet. Losing 20 pounds should not be your only motive to start moving. Regular physical activity should be as important to you as brushing your teeth or getting a mammogram. Taking care of your body by allowing it to move is your responsibility.

If you get enough physical activity every day, you will burn more calories. But more importantly, you'll feel better and your perception of food can even change. Exercise is a great catalyst for other healthy behaviors. You start to experience the "feel good" advantage of exercise and it spills over into other areas of your lifestyle. Regular exercise is uplifting to the spirit and can reduce emotional eating and stress, increase your mental capabilities, make you feel good about yourself, and reduce or eliminate mild depression.

Some studies say that for many cases of depression, physical activity and healthy eating habits are more effective than anti-depressants. The unfortunate reality is that in today's drug-dependent environment, anti-anxiety and anti-depressant medications are some of most widely used prescriptions. The most interesting findings are that most psychiatrists aren't dispensing the prescriptions for diagnosis and treatment of a chemical imbalance; rather, the primary care physician is dispensing them. A patient comes in with symptoms such as chronic headaches, difficulty sleeping, fatigue, back or neck pain, weight gain, depression or stress, and the patient is given a prescription. Only the prescription doesn't solve the problem, it just masks the symptoms.

Think of physical activity as treatment for a "lifestyle imbalance," instead of a chemical imbalance. A change in lifestyle can prevent the need for the medication, and most likely, be more effective.

I thought this particular study from Duke University would be good to share with you. There were 53 participants, who were first instructed to be inactive for six months, and then were physically active for six months. Afterwards, the researchers reported on the measurements they took before and after. Here is an excerpt from their findings:

> The researchers measured 17 biological factors known to increase cardiovascular risk, including waist size, physical fitness, visceral fat levels, body mass index, cholesterol levels, insulin sensitivity and indicators of metabolic syndrome, a precursor of diabetes.
>
> "In the analysis, we found that waist size, time to exhaustion, visceral fat and metabolic syndrome scores deteriorated significantly during the six-month period of inactivity during the original trial. However, after six months of exercise training in

the study, 13 of the 17 variables had either reverted to original baseline levels or even improved."

According to the study, only a moderate amount of exercise (the study measured many different levels of exercise, "moderate" measured at 12 miles per week) is needed to counteract the detrimental effects of inactivity in these individuals.

"When looking at the group as a whole, we found it wasn't the participants with the highest intensity of exercise who accounted for the combined beneficial effects. That should be reassuring for people to know they don't have to do a high-intensity workout to get these benefits of exercise."

Twelve miles a week is less than two miles a day. This basic requirement is very simple to meet and its benefit is so indisputable. One has to wonder why anyone would resist accomplishing this small contribution to personal health.

BE THANKFUL!

There are so many people in this world who are disabled through no fault of their own and would give anything to be able to walk, ride a bike or move their bodies freely. Yet, many who are so fortunate to have the gift of an able body don't appreciate it and don't take care of it. Just as with getting better nutrition, it is your responsibility to take care of yourself by getting regular physical activity. Moving your body shouldn't have to be a burden, but a joy!

WHY WE DON'T DO IT

When I interview my clients as to why they don't take the time to move their bodies daily, the excuses start flowing. As I said earlier in the book, if you rely on excuses you will never be successful. So, let's talk about getting rid of excuses that are mental obstacles to listening to our bodies' desire to move.

I DON'T HAVE TIME!

Of course, this is the most popular excuse, and for the most part, with good reason. We are busier these days, and fitting a regular time slot for exercise into a hectic schedule can almost seem frivolous in the face of the demands of life. But, maybe you just aren't recognizing how important it really is. I mean, if taking time to move your body daily helps you to be healthier, have more energy, reduce stress, feel better, sleep better... don't you think that's pretty important and should be at the top of your list of things to do? The reality is that everything you do you will do better if you take care of yourself first. You will be a better partner, parent, professional and friend. It's like the oxygen mask dropping from the airplane. You are instructed to put the mask on yourself before you help others.

We look at taking time for ourselves as a luxury after we have gotten everything else done, and then some – when in reality, it is a necessity, to enable us to get everything else done effectively and efficiently.

The Real Truth

I did a little experiment with a group of eight women who cited lack of time as a reason for not getting physical activity. I asked them to commit to doing 50 push-ups every day for seven days. They could do them military style, on their knees, or against a wall – whatever their capacity. They could do them 10 at a time, 20 at a time, or all at once. Just do it. Not a single person accomplished this small task every day. The combined daily time to execute 50 push-ups is less than 3 minutes.

Now, you would have to be one seriously busy person to not have three minutes a day. The reality is that it's not about having the actual time, it's about mental barriers – making it too complicated, making excuses, having blinders, or the rigid dieting mindset that physical activity needs to be timed, structured and goal-oriented to be beneficial. Citing lack of time is just an easier way of giving in to these other obstacles.

Where Are YOU On Your List of Things To Do?

Often, we start out our day and put ourselves at the top of our list of things to do, but as the day goes on, we allow everyone and everything to get in the way of taking care of ourselves. Our needs fall right off the list. I think the reason for this is mostly because we feel our needs are not as important as others'. Moms, especially, are vulnerable to this selflessness. We do for others, but not for ourselves.

You need to decide how important taking care of your physical and mental needs is going to be for you. If you make it a priority, you will get it done, just as you do everything else that you deem important.

I ask clients to write down the top three things they need to do every day, and put themselves on that list. If they don't take time for themselves because "everything else" got in the way, I ask them to honestly take a look at their day and see how many far less important things got in the way.

Think about this: How important is watching your favorite TV show? What items on your list do you forego because the TV show is so important? Or, how efficiently do you get your tasks done so that you can spare the time to sit and enjoy your program? Now, consider how important you view taking care of your mental and physical health and feeling better.

Everything Else But

We tend to spend more time thinking about exercise than actually doing it. Sometimes the reason so many things get in the way is because we procrastinate. It's next on our list and we may have the time, but we will purposefully do this or that before we get ready to put our bodies in motion. If you have to pick up your son at 3:00 from school, you can't think, "Oh, I'll pick him up at 3:30 instead." If you have a busy day, pick a time and then try to stick with it. If you plan to take that walk after work, come in, change your clothes, put your shoes on and get out the door – don't linger and wait for three other things to get in the way.

If you make plans to go to the gym directly after work, don't dawdle – getting your final duties done until you look at the clock and say, "Oh well, too late, don't have time to go to the gym now." Make a commitment to leave at 5:00 and then get it done – just as if you had to leave for a meeting (certain exceptions noted).

We Make It Too Complicated

The timed, structured, goal-oriented view of exercise allows excuses to get in the way. If you need an hour and a half to get to the gym or take a class, a lot can get in the way. If you feel like you have to workout for a certain period of time in order for it to "do anything," and anything else is a waste of time, then things will get in the way.

The fact is that anything is better than nothing. Studies are showing that if you exercise for just 10 minutes 3 times a day, it is almost as beneficial as 30 minutes all at once. Even if you only got in 10 minutes a day, you would feel a bit better, get your heart to work harder and burn a few calories.

Avoiding Movement

Most of us are oblivious to how much we resist moving. We go out of our way to minimize our movement, sometimes even causing us to take more time to complete a task. Here are a few of my observations:

- We wait minutes longer for an elevator when we could have taken the stairs.

- While there may be 10 cars in line at the drive-thru, there are often only 2 people in line in the restaurant. Why? Because people would rather sit in a line than get out of their car to go into the restaurant. So much for fast food and time management. I had a client who ate nearly every meal at the drive-thru. My first instruction to him was to start walking into the restaurant. He fought me on this, until we uncovered that in addition to his avoiding movement by going into the restaurant, he had to acknowledge his actions more. The reality was he felt uncomfortable ordering his super-sized meal in person because he was so overweight, whereas in the drive-thru, there is anonymity and one can easily put up blinders.

♦ Instinctively, we pull into the front of the Walmart or Target, where inevitably we wait for pedestrians, and we wait for the car in front of us who is waiting for a parking space and then we make our way up and down the parking aisles until we find our perfect spot. All of this takes a lot of time and can be very stressful and annoying – especially when all we want to do is get home and relax! Here's a better way. Pull into the back of the parking lot and make your way forward. Find the first spot that is open and whip in. Move briskly or even jog into the store, bypassing that guy who was in front of you who is still waiting for pedestrians to cross, and make your way into the store. By doing this you have not only accomplished your task faster, but you have burned more calories and the ordeal is far less stressful.

I'M TOO TIRED!

"I'm too tired" is the second most popular excuse. But what is tired? If you spent six hours doing yard work, or work as a waitperson, landscaper or other labor-intensive job, you really might be tired. But, if you have been at a desk all day, all your body wants to do is get up, stretch and move around. If you come home, eat and then lie on the couch watching TV, surfing the Net or reading a book, you're not in touch with your body's needs.

As with our food behavior, when contemplating exercise, we tend to listen to our mind, not our body. You can be mentally exhausted, but your body might be screaming to move! If you've had a stressed out, busy day, you may think the last thing you need is to take a walk, or do some calisthenics. Typically, the more stressed and mentally tired you are, the more beneficial the physical activity.

Signs Your Body Wants to Move

Are you restless? Are you feeling down? Are you irritable? Do you have trouble sleeping at night? Are you always feeling tired? Are you stiff when you get up off the couch? Do you move slowly? Are you always cold and wanting to curl up with a blanket? These are signs that your body needs more movement. Unfortunately, many of these symptoms are what we use as our excuses not to move.

Motivation Isn't Magical

If your thoughts are steering you in the direction of the comfy couch, the thought of exercising is grueling. I feel your pain. People who engage in regular physical activity don't just magically get up and exercise freely. You still have the hesitation. However, once we've experienced a physically active lifestyle, even though the couch is always an option, we choose to get off of it because we want to feel good, happier, more energetic and enjoy life more. It's like a wonder drug. Your mental capabilities, creativity, mood and energy level can change in 20 minutes of walking in the fresh air. Why would you want to resist such a benefit?

Once you get into the habit of getting regular exercise, you will appreciate the great feeling afterwards and the thought of not doing it overrides the negative initial feelings of doing it. The "I'll-do-it-tomorrow" attitude diminishes when you recognize the immediate negative outcome of that decision. The decision is not about the total number of calories you are going to burn, but deciding how you want to feel going forward.

Think About How You Will Feel Afterward

When our focus is on the goal of weight loss – our reward doesn't come until somewhere down the road, so we hurry up and try to drive there. We try to lose 10 pounds by making ourselves miserable trying to do too much, too soon. Then we give up. "This is too hard! It's not working. Why bother?" Focus not on how you feel before you get started, but how you will feel when you are done – relaxed, proud of yourself and in a better mood. I've never known of anyone who said, "Gee, I wish I didn't exercise."

GETTING STARTED IS THE HARDEST PART

The biggest hurdle is getting started. If you're having trouble getting off the couch, try breaking down what you are trying to accomplish into smaller parts. For example, say you've committed yourself to walking for two miles and you're sitting on the couch thinking, "I don't want to walk two miles." Instead, break down the goal into parts and accomplish them one at a time. Like this:

First Goal: Get off the couch. Take a stretch, yawn.

Second Goal: Get your shoes on, etc.

Third Goal: Go outside (just to get some fresh air, I can come back in if I want).

Final Goal: Start walking.

Once you get started, the rest is easy. By the time you've made it around the block, walking two miles doesn't seem like such an effort. In fact, not only will you most likely enjoy it, you may even be motivated to do more!

If your plan is to get to the gym or to an exercise class, don't think that you are too tired to work out. Just get in the car and get there. Once you are there, and the activity is in motion, the rest is easy.

Here's a true personal example of "just getting started." I spend a lot of time at my computer. After a few hours of this sedentary, brain stimulating activity, my eyes will burn, I feel tired and I start zoning out. My body feels cold. Sometimes I will wrap myself in a blanket. I feel my mental energy decline and I almost get this depressed feeling. When I get this way, I take a break and move my body, even though the last thing I want to do is get up. But I know if I do, I will feel so much better, my brain will be rejuvenated, I will get more accomplished and I will feel good again.

On this particular day, it's raining, so I have to rely on the treadmill. I get up. I grab my sneakers – I'm so lazy, I don't even put them on. With blanket on, I go upstairs and step on the treadmill. In my Crocs and wearing a blanket, I hit the big red button and begin walking at a two mph speed. Yawning, I flip the channel changer. Three minutes later I'm getting warm, and I shed the blanket. At four minutes, I stop and put my sneakers on. I get back on and increase the speed to three mph. As I get warmer, I peel off the sweatshirt. By 10 minutes I have worked my way into my "zone," put on my iPod and start getting into it. As I'm bopping to the beat, I start thinking about the project I'm working on, sorting things out, thinking of a good strategy.

By 30 minutes, I'm done. I feel awesome! My body is warmed up, my muscles relaxed, my mental energy is renewed, and I feel good about myself. Back to work with a whole new attitude, fresh ideas and so glad I took that one small step to such a big reward for myself!

WHAT TO DO THAT'S BEST FOR YOU

Choosing your physical activity of choice should be based on what you like to do, your physical condition and/or limitations, your budget and your time constraints. It's also great to have a variety of interests. Take up challenging hiking trails on weekends, with neighborhood walks during the week. Combine walking, a once a week dance class, along with a few days of two 10-minute calisthenic workouts at home. Do strength training three days and walking two days. Just be open to any opportunity for movement. Find ways to work any of these options into your busy schedule, even if it's only a few minutes at a time. The more the better, even something is better than nothing!

Joining a Gym

If you are interested in joining a gym, realistically consider if you have enough flexibility in your life to routinely get there. Otherwise, the gym will do you more harm than good because not having time to go the gym can be a very valid excuse. If you decide to join a gym, I recommend that you still have a back-up plan at home as an option. So, even if you only get to the gym once or twice that week, you are able to fill in with some activity on days you can't get there.

Before you join a gym, demonstrate to yourself that you are committed to making exercise a habit by doing a physical activity on a regular basis first. Make sure you have overcome the resistance to "just doing it" before you spend your hard-earned money on a gym membership.

At-Home Equipment

There are hundreds of gadgets and different types of equipment to help you achieve physical fitness. Some are great, others a big waste of money. We often want to buy the equipment that is going to get us the results we want the fastest. The reality is, they all work as long as you use them consistently! You are the one who is exerting the energy. So, whether it's a treadmill, a stair climber, a cross trainer or bike, it will give the results of the energy you put into it. Consider the space you have, the cost, and your ability to use the equipment and choose the one you will enjoy using the most.

The Treadmill

When in doubt, get a treadmill. It is the most versatile piece of equipment. It can accommodate nearly all levels of physical fitness. You can walk at two mph or run at eight. If you aren't a runner but want more of a challenge, you can use the incline for an intense workout without the jarring effects of running. It's also great for the whole family, from your eight-year-old to your grandmother. Put it in front of the TV right in the family room if that's what it takes to use it. The more accessible and comfortable the placement, the more likely you will use it. Make deals with yourself. "I can't watch the Phillies game unless I agree to spend 30 minutes on the treadmill." Even if it's just at two mph, it's better than lying on the couch.

If you have overweight children, a treadmill is a great negotiating tool to increase activity. Lay down the rule that they can't watch their muntant ninja cartoon unless they are on the treadmill!

SAY YES! TO WEIGHT TRAINING

The benefits of incorporating regular weight training into your life are immeasurable. Weight training increases metabolism, builds and retains muscle mass, assists in adding and keeping bone density, protects bones from injury, helps keep and improve your posture and figure, and is mentally empowering. Weight training keeps your body young. I am a huge proponent of weight training and I hope to give you some compelling reasons to inspire and motivate you to take up this hugely beneficial activity. It's easy to incorporate into anyone's busy lifestyle.

You Can Eat More

It takes about 40 calories to feed a pound of muscle versus 2–5 calories to feed a pound of fat. If you gain three pounds of muscle, you theoretically could eat nearly 150 more calories a day and still maintain your weight.

This has a profound effect as we age. The older we get, the harder it is to retain lean muscle. Our bodies get flabby, and we can't seem to eat as much as we used to and still maintain our weight. Women, especially, lose muscle dramatically during menopause. Weight training can inhibit the effects of this reality and not only provide health benefits, but help you keep your youthful appearance and increase your metabolism.

A Pound of Muscle is More Dense than Fat

Many people will incorrectly say that a pound of fat weighs more than a pound of muscle, which is silly because a pound is a pound is a pound, right? However, a pound of muscle is smaller, but heavier. So, if you have an extra two pounds of muscle in your butt, your butt will be smaller than if you have two pounds of fat in your butt.

Because of this reality, personal trainers' biggest frustration is the huge difficulty they face when trying to convince clients to take their eyes off of the scale and start looking in the mirror, or to pay attention to how their clothes fit. If you are following a comprehensive combination of good nutrition, calorie balance, exercise and weight training, the powerful end result of weight loss and muscle gain will be achieved.

Sculpt a Great Body

While you cannot spot-reduce fat, you can increase muscle mass in various areas of your body. As you are shedding fat through calorie control and exercise, you can transform your shape through weight training. Have an apple shape? Work on your legs to create a shapelier butt, and work your back to stand straighter and reduce the pooch. Pear shaped? Work on upper body to build shoulder definition and create more symmetry with your lower body. For men, if you want to get rid of the beer gut, work your entire body, focusing on your weaker areas. Abdominal work helps, but will not get you results unless you build muscle and include good nutrition and regular exercise.

Getting Started

Weight training can easily be done in the home with just a few dumbbells and an exercise ball or a weight bench. Many resistance exercises can be done using your own body weight, and no equipment is needed at all.

What to Do

If you want to incorporate weight training into your life, I strongly suggest you get educated. Improperly executing movements can lead to injury. Not understanding the mechanics of which exercise applies to what muscle can be ineffective use of your time. Invest in a few training sessions with a recommended fitness professional. Many provide services in your home and can help you create your own in-home program with limited space and equipment.

Change It Up

Once you have basic education on weight training, you can develop your own program that incorporates strength-training movements with cardiovascular components (jog in place, jumping jacks, etc.) for an intense workout in the convenience of your own home.

An alternative is to simply work in 10 minutes a day and focus on a particular body part at a time. I am famous for multi-tasking my strength training by doing bicep workouts while cooking dinner –12 curls, stir the pot, 12 more curls, set the table . . . adding my daily walks with the dogs to round out my activity routine.

FITTING BURSTS OF ENERGY INTO YOUR LIFE

A study from Iowa State University found that obese women stood for two hours less than their lean counterparts – a simple habit researchers say could make a difference of 300 calories a day. Being aware of this potential pitfall can help you outsmart it. Standing for an hour or more a day—at your desk, in the doctor's waiting room, or at your kids' soccer game will burn 100 more calories than if you were sitting, says Darcy Johannsen, Ph.D., R.D.

Keeping this in mind, here are many activities you can do to burn calories and get lean and healthy:

- Get an exercise ball and bounce or roll around on it while watching TV

- Calisthenics: jumping jacks, lunges, hill climbers, push-ups, jog in place. Basic military body movements can provide an awesome workout that can be done in short bursts of just a few minutes to long duration workouts.

- Watch a Cable Fitness show and try some of the moves

- Turn on the music and dance

- Weight train

- Learn boxing and kicking movements

- Periodically walk up or down stairs

- Walk the long way

- Play with your kids

- Walk your dog

- Walk around your house perimeter and check out your plants, pull weeds, etc.

STEP IT UP!

Sometimes the difference between being thin or heavy can be simply how we move day-to-day. Many of us move slowly. Watch yourself move. Do you shuffle or do you stride? How about the stairs? Do you run or walk up, stair by stair? How quickly do you get out of the car and into a store?

If you can be open to movement and take advantage of opportunities to move more frequently throughout the day, you could work off the equivalent of a 20-minute treadmill walk in a day. Just putting a little spring in your step can help.

MULTI-TASK YOUR TIME

Combine conversations with walking. Take a walk with your kids or your spouse instead of sitting at the kitchen counter. Walking is a great stress reliever and can lead to many more constructive conversations. Some employers are now allowing employees to do walking meetings, as a way to combine physical activity with work productivity. Here are some other ideas:

- Postpone your weekly phone call to your aging mother? Bring your cell phone on a walk and you can pull duty while taking care of your body.

- If you are waiting at the copy machine, do wall pushups or stretching.

♦ If your kids play sports, don't just sit there for two hours watching. Take frequent walks around the field or use a nearby running track.

OPPORTUNITIES ARE EVERYWHERE

Take a look around you and see how easy it is to put more movement into your life. And, if you have already done your planned exercise for the day, don't pass up the opportunity to do more – take advantage of it.

PROGRESS MAKES PERFECT

Once you get in the habit of adding physical activity into your life, you may find that you want to challenge yourself. Interval training is a great way to increase your endurance, without torturing yourself in the process.

For example, let's say you've been walking three miles, five days a week and you would like to try jogging. To increase intensity, during your walk, practice short jogging or running sprints. For example, tell yourself, "I'm going to run from here to the third mailbox." When you successfully reach your goal, start walking again. You'll feel winded, as your heart rate has elevated. Try it again a few minutes later, and you will find the next sprint easier than the first because your starting heart rate is a little higher. Do this consistently and you may find yourself a few months later running in a 5K race! You may be surprised at what you can do.

OTHER BENEFITS OF PHYSICAL ACTIVITY

Settle your stomach

If we have overeaten or have indigestion, our inactive self tends to head towards the couch for relief. Lying down actually aggravates the problem by washing stomach acids into the esophagus causing heartburn. Light physical activity like walking is the best remedy. The movement helps digest the food, break up the gas and burn some of the excess calories as well.

Great PMS remedy

If you have bloat, cramping, and aches and pains, inactivity does nothing to help the symptoms. If you get up and start moving, you will find that your symptoms actually subside and you will feel better.

Ease arthritis pain

The best way to relieve general arthritis pain symptoms is to move; the worst thing is not to move. I had an 87-year-old neighbor who lived on the corner in a small bungalow on two acres of land all by herself. She amazed me. I'd see her out there raking leaves, mowing the grass with a push mower, and moving wood. I stopped one day just to tell her how proud I was of her. I found out that she also walks six miles every morning with her "gentleman friend." When my jaw dropped, she said, "Oh my goodness, I have to keep moving! With my arthritis, if I stop, I'll never start again!"

ARE YOU CONVINCED?

If you have been struggling with getting yourself to commit to physical activity, I hope I have given you motivation, a compelling reason to change, and ideas on how to accomplish your objective. Sometimes we just think too much about it. Moving your body is instinctive and, for many reasons, we have resisted giving in to that instinct. Once you get into the habit of responding to those instincts again through conscious decisions, your body will start responding too, and the benefit will far outweigh the effort you have to put into it. Moving your body will be a natural part of your new lifestyle – a joyous part that makes you feel better and leads you to a better quality of life.

Get Moving

Moving your body doesn't have to be planned, timed or structured. Just get up and do something!

- Putting the activity in motion is the hardest part – break it down into easy steps

- Be thankful for the gift of mobility, and respect it

- Make physical activity a necessary part of good health – just like brushing your teeth

- With physical activity the less you do, the less you want to do; the more you do, the more you want to do

- Consider getting educated in weight training to keep your metabolism revved and keep yourself looking younger

- If you feel tired, but haven't moved your body much, it's your brain that is tired – your body is probably screaming to move

- Make physical activity a joyous part of your life – not a sacrifice

12

Be Aware of Your Stress

*I*n today's environment, stress has become an influential part of our daily lives. While stress is inevitable, chronic stress can be debilitating – even life threatening. Many of us are living in a state of chronic stress and it has become not only acceptable, but also expected. And just like the foods we eat and how we move our body, if stress is impacting the quality of your life, you owe it to yourself, and everyone around you, to take steps to manage it.

Most of us are "in it" and have considered stress just a part of our daily lives. We know we are stressed, we even laugh about it. We just react to it, not realizing the negative effect it is having on our health, our relationships, our work product and happiness. We don't view it as something we need to change. We just accept it as normal.

Chronic stress leads to emotional eating, depression, and sleep disorders, and can actually cause physical illness. Some research says that up to 50 percent of preventable illness is stress related and it inhibits our bodies' resistance to colds, flu and other ailments.

EVOLUTION OF STRESS

It's easy to see why we have so much stress in our lives. Technology has profoundly impacted our lives. We live in a fast paced, "I need it now" world. People in the business environment have become slaves to emails meetings, voicemail and the 24-hour world of technology. I once watched a businessman walk into a wall reading his email on a Blackberry at an airport. Years ago, when you needed written correspondence, the US Mail was our vehicle for delivery. You spent your work time getting a proposal together, put it in the mail and waited two weeks before you had to even look at it again, and in the meantime you would move on to your next project. Today, you send the proposal via email and sometimes within minutes, you get a response asking for this or that. It's as though it never leaves your desk and seems to go on endlessly. Some people I've talked to can get up to 50 emails or more a day – how can you possibly answer every single one and still have time to get your work done? As a former corporate employee, I can remember times when I would start my mornings with a two-hour meeting that didn't accomplish anything; go back to a dozen emails and respond to everyone all day long; and then do my actual work load at home.

Education has become a stressor. Thirty years ago you could climb the corporate ladder with a little gumption, common sense and dedication. A college degree was a luxury and not a necessity to get ahead. Today, even community colleges are not good enough, as companies seek out only the few who had the benefit of a top college education. And no sooner do you get your career off the ground than you're back in school, studying for your Masters so you can get ahead. Only now, instead of being in a college frat house, you have a full-time job and two children at home. And, we start worrying about paying for our kids' education before they are even out of the womb.

Our workdays are longer and most of us travel further to get to work. Almost two million people commute 90 minutes or longer door-to-door. Years ago, retail stores were closed on Sunday and corporate workdays used to be nine to five. Today we have 24-hour retail and traffic jams start as early as 6:30 am. And once you left work, you came home to dinner at six, your pipe and slippers and the evening paper. Not to take care of everything else that didn't get done because no one was home all day.

I'm going down a slippery path here and, okay, maybe a bit too much Ozzie and Harriet again. But the reality is that life was simpler when Mom was home to manage the house, children, shopping and other responsibilities during the day, so that the evenings were a time to relax.

But since the burning of the bra in the 60's, women have been evolving into superwomen and they have proven themselves worthy more than anyone could have envisioned. Unfortunately, many who are achieving it all are not very good at delegating anything, and end up doing it all as well. And I don't mean to forget the men. Men's stress levels are escalating as well, as they try to deal with the chaos and dual roles. Life is so hectic, and there is so much conflict, it causes relationships to be frail and libido to dwindle. As we try to manage the family, work and community, we not only forget to take care of ourselves, but we forget to take care of each other as well.

So many women, especially single moms (and I don't mean to imply just women) work full-time at their jobs and have the same responsibilities as a full-time housewife. Not only are they adapting to the added stress of technology and increasing workload, they are filling the role of housekeeper, chef, financial manager and taxicab driver. To make matters worse, our expected responsibilities as parents have gotten out of control. So now, we are not only facing more stress at work, and a dual role as house manager, but also now we are expected to sit on soccer fields and man concession stands most evenings and weekends. Some families travel several hours (even overnight) for weekend competitions and their children's age hasn't even hit the double digits yet.

I have just scratched the surface of the changes in our world. I could dedicate a whole book on observations of the evolution of stress (and there are probably a few good books out there that do). While I speak of the negative, there is a lot of positive to go along with it as well. I support both a woman's right to pursue her professional goals, and the right to choose to put her goals on hold to spend more time with her children. And, most women are living more fulfilling lives. Along with a lot of frustration, there is a lot of satisfaction. In many ways all our lives and society are better off. So, the answer is not to send Mom back into the kitchen. (Of course, maybe Dad would rather be in the kitchen).

And maybe even if you wanted to change the family dynamics, most of us couldn't because we have a lot of expenses and feel we are one step away from a pink slip.

IT'S NOT GOING TO GO AWAY

With the reality of our crazy world, it's not like we can just quit our jobs and start basket weaving on a Caribbean island. So, how do you do it all? Honestly, it has gotten to the point where at times you can't. Sometimes you can only do your best, and your best has to be good enough or you will go crazy. But while you may not be able to change your environment, there are ways to survive happily in spite of it. Just like eating better and moving your body, you can manage your stress by taking steps to recognize it and make it important enough to do something about it.

As the final component to your journey to a better life, we're going to examine the impact stress may be having on your well-being as a whole. By identifying your major stressors and the effect they may be having on your life, you can figure out what you can do to manage them better. Rather than just running on the gerbil wheel going and going, we're going to take a step back to figure out what stressors are most negatively impacting your life, and take steps to lessen that impact. Ways to manage stress include taking better care of yourself, getting rested sleep, changing attitudes, dealing with conflict, and even delegating and organization.

LOOK AT YOUR LIFE HOLISTICALLY

The word "holistic" scares people, as historically it has been referenced as some New Age-hippie-type-way of living favored by yoga devotees and granola people. But because the impact of stress has gotten so out of control, total wellness solutions are embracing the holistic way of thinking. To view your life holistically simply means contemplating your total self, as it is proven that each component of mind, body and spirit is interconnected, and this enables one to achieve harmony.

Understanding the impact that each component has on your overall well-being allows you to consider what you may need in order to truly experience a better quality of life. Taking care of yourself, including managing stress, provides you with the ammunition you need to take on the demands of your day-to-day life.

WHAT IS YOUR STRESS LEVEL?

Stress is a fact of life. In fact, not all stress is bad. Positive stress gives us excitement, it gives us momentum and keeps our lives fulfilling. If we had no stress in our lives, it would be pretty boring. The problem is, when stress builds or when negative stress is ongoing, we can get into a state of chronic stress. Chronic stress occurs when we are experiencing continuous stress over a long period of time, and it is negatively impacting the quality of our work, our mood, our health and our happiness. And when something distressful happens – such as divorce, death or losing a job on top of chronic stress, there is no capacity left to deal with it. Too many of us are near our capacity just coping with our daily lives, let alone having to deal with a distressful situation.

One of my topics as a motivational speaker is to address stress during the holidays. Our lives are already stressed out, and when we pack on the duties of getting ready for the holidays as well, it can send some of us over the edge. Instead of the holidays being the time to be spiritual and experience joy and appreciation, we get downright angry. Some of us despise that time of year and are miserable.

WHAT ARE THE MAJOR STRESSORS IN YOUR LIFE?

Think about what situations or issues in your life are causing you the most stress. It could be financial problems, relationships, conflict or illness in the family. What weighs on you most? Takes up most of your time? Not only in actual time, but takes up space in your brain – distracts you the most. You may find that you have several major stressors in your life.

WHAT IMPACT IS STRESS HAVING ON YOU?

Stress can negatively impact your physical, mental and emotional well-being, and can be the root cause of such debilitating conditions as headache, fatigue, sleeplessness, depression, irritability, anxiety, weight gain or loss, forgetfulness and difficulty making decisions.

Consider if any of the major stressors in your life could be causing or aggravating these symptoms. If you are experiencing a lot of these symptoms, then it is time to take action and do something about it.

WHAT TO DO ABOUT IT

Once you have identified the stressors and their impact on your life, you can hopefully understand their importance, and you will be motivated to do something about it. While you may not be able to change stressful situations in your life, there is a lot you can do to control them.

CHANGE YOUR ATTITUDE

Stress is mostly about perception. How we perceive the situation has a lot to do with how we react to it. When we are feeling stressed, we can change our outlook on things. When we have chronic stress, our attitude can become negative and our personality can change. We just don't feel right. We get upset easily, blow things out of proportion and lose perception of what is really happening. We are caught in traffic and it's the end of the world, when, in reality it's just normal occurrences in our day-to-day life. One day your child spills her milk and you say, "That's okay sweetie, accidents happen." The next time she does it and you are stressed out you may say, "Damn it, why are you always so clumsy? This is all I need right now!" What further aggravates things is that when we react unreasonably to a situation, we usually feel bad about it and start carrying guilt on top of everything else.

While stressful situations can't be avoided, you can change your reaction to them by simply thinking things through for a moment instead of just acting out. Taking a deep breath, looking at the situation in the big picture of life can give you time to put things in perspective. Getting angry at uncontrollable situations only takes up space in your brain and adds unnecessary stress to your life.

I know this is easier said than done, but changing your attitude does work. It's a mindset. Once you take a deep breath and accept what is realistically happening, your stress level decreases. The old sayings, "Count to 10" and "Don't sweat the small stuff" are very good pieces of advice for changing perspective.

BEING OVERWHELMED

When we have too much going on at one time, our brain doesn't respond well. We can't organize our thoughts enough to complete the tasks at hand. We get easily distracted, waste time worrying about how much we have to do, and can't focus on actually doing it. Anxiety mounts and we start freaking out. When this happens, you have to first recognize that you are overwhelmed and then slow yourself down, gather your thoughts, prioritize, focus and finish. "Focus and finish" is a mantra I learned from a very organized colleague of mine and I use it faithfully. It's about taking on tasks one at a time, keeping distractions at bay until you can finish the task. So, if it means turning off your email alert or closing your door, or telling your kids they have to keep themselves occupied until Mommy or Daddy's done, then do it. And when you find your mind leading you to distractions of worry and daydreaming, a mental reminder of focus and finish can help get you back on track.

MANAGING OUR PRIORITIES

Most of us are not very good at managing our life. A good manager will prioritize, eliminate and delegate. Make sure you get the most important things done first, eliminate what is not necessary, and delegate tasks that can be done by others. For example, if you have a family and a professional life to take care of, what are your most important responsibilities? Probably, in this order: 1) your family, 2) your personal needs (if you follow this book), 3) your job, and then 4) everything else. So, where does that leave keeping your house spotless, getting your nails done, watching the game or surfing the Internet? Pretty far down on the list.

DELEGATING

Many of us don't delegate well, which adds to our list of things to do and can lead to resentment. Ironically (and typically), the more overwhelmed we are, the more reluctant we are to delegate. We start working in a tunnel never looking up to see if there is a lifeline to grab onto. Is there a coworker who has offered to help you with your project? Are you running around doing laundry at night while your teenage kids are playing video games? Instead of delegating, we get resentful and huff "I have to do everything myself!"

Give clear direction

If you want someone to do a task for you, make sure you have instructed them on how you want it done. Don't complain that the person you delegated didn't do it right if you didn't let them know your expectations as to what to accomplish and when.

Let go of perfection

Sometimes we are reluctant to delegate because we know we will do it better or someone will complete the task differently or not as efficiently. Accept that it doesn't have to be "your way" and lighten up on your insistence of perfection.

Let others know it's important to you

Understand that what you view as important may not be important to others. The laundry basket hasn't been sitting at the bottom of the stairs for two days because everyone just expects someone else to do it for them. They may simply not care that it's there and so they don't even notice it – it's not important to them. However, if they understood that it was their responsibility to carry it upstairs and it was important to you, they would be more likely to do it. With children, it could take several times for it to sink in, but if you're persistent, or if there was a penalty or reward for their actions, they would get the job done.

JUST SAY NO

Often we create our overwhelming situations by deliberately taking on more than we can handle. Over-achievers suffer from stress the most, because they are always the one willing to step up and take responsibility – and they do it willingly and with the best of intentions. However, if they don't set boundaries, they can ultimately take on too many responsibilities and the stress builds and overwhelms them.

Before you raise your hand to take on another project, community event or party planning, think about what you have on your plate and if it's already full, save yourself by putting your hand down and saying "No" to any more commitments. If you keep your hand down long enough, someone else will raise theirs. Save yourself.

KEEP JOY IN YOUR LIFE

When we are in a state of chronic stress we can lose our sense of joy. We can't let our hair down and have fun because we are so wound up we can't relax. There is no time for fun. Remember, in spite of your hectic life, you have to bear in mind what life is all about and the reason you are here.

TAKE CARE OF YOURSELF

Since this book is all about taking care of yourself, I won't go into detail here, except to point out again that your best defense against stress getting the best of you is taking care of your personal needs.

The problem is that the more stressed out we are, the more likely we are to not take care of ourselves and, instead, take care of everyone and everything else first. You will be better able to take on everyone and everything else if you take care of yourself first. For the most part, people who successfully lead the busiest, most stressful lives make sure they take care of their physical and mental needs in order to better take on the demands of their life.

Meditation

Meditation is a useful tool to help manage the mental challenges of stress. It isn't something you have to do in a yoga position, with your fingertips up in the air for 20 minutes, ahmmming (although it's pretty cool to do). Just giving yourself some quiet time to reflect, appreciate or just organize your thoughts can help. You can Google many sites that will give instruction on meditation or try to attend a class.

RESOLVE CONFLICT

Many of us walk around with conflict looming over us – conflict with coworkers, family, friends, even ourselves. Conflict takes up space in the brain; it distracts us, brings us down and gets in the way of our joy. Employees leave jobs because they can't get along with their boss or a coworker. Family arguments at Thanksgiving turn into years of silence, and people get divorced without ever seeking counseling.

If you have conflict that is taking up space in your brain, resolve it. If you can't deal directly with the individual you're in conflict with, then seek a mediator or counselor.

I'm sure you've had this experience: You had a spat with your spouse, partner or child and it upsets you the rest of the day. You play it over and over again in your head, you can't focus at work, you're down or you feel angry. Then you get home, kiss and make up, and then it's like this great weight is lifted off of you and you feel good again. Chronic conflict with others adds to our overall stress, and can be crippling to our happiness and productivity.

Communication

Many of us do not know how to express our feelings in a non-threatening or constructive way. Family counseling can help not only in time of crisis, but communication skills learned through counseling can be used to keep families' lines of communication open, enabling family members to keep in touch with each others' needs and feelings. Good communication with others can give you a great sense of peace and harmony.

SLEEP

According to the National Sleep foundation, almost 74 percent of Americans do not get enough sleep each night. We sleep on average an hour less a night than we did 20 years ago. Our bodies need sleep for repair and if they don't get it, our bodies can't defend themselves – and we are more vulnerable to illness. Lack of sleep impedes our mental performance and contributes to depression, anxiety and traffic accidents.

As stress levels get higher, our sleeping patterns get worse. And this, of course, at a time when we need sleep even more to take on the demands of our hectic lives. We go to bed at night with the day's events and our next day's calendar spinning around in our heads, and we can't relax enough to drift off into a sound, restful sleep. Not having enough sleep also contributes to emotional eating and lack of exercise.

If you are one of the millions who suffer from sleep deprivation, take action to do something about it. Here are a few tips:

Start your nightly routine earlier

Are you the type that announces you are going to bed at 10:30 – only to stop and fold the laundry, kiss the kids good night (followed by a 15 minute conversation about a girl friend), read the mail, pick out your clothes for the next day and then wind up catching the end of Conan O'Brien's monologue? You finally turn out the lights and it's midnight and your alarm is set for 5:30. Then you lie there, staring at the ceiling fretting because, once again, you aren't going to get enough sleep. If this frequently happens to you, then accept that the "good night" process takes over an hour, and factor that into your planned bedtime.

Move your body daily

As we previously discussed, often our brains are exhausted, but our bodies are restless. If you sat most of the day, you may find that your body is fidgety when trying to sleep. Physical activity will not only help your body rest, but will relieve some mental stress and relax your mind as well.

Don't overeat or eat late at night

While you never want to go to bed hungry, if you try to sleep on a full stomach, you will most likely regret it. By lying down on a full stomach you may find yourself with acid in-digestion and sleep disruption.

THE MIND/BODY CONNECTION

So, when contemplating your lifestyle actions – what you eat, how you eat, why you eat and how you move or don't move – also consider the impact stress may have on your life. Unmanaged stress could be contributing to difficulty in achieving your other lifestyle goals. By taking better care of yourself through eating well and getting regular physical activity and adequate amounts of sleep, you will be better able to manage the stress in your life. By identifying the mind-body connection you will achieve a better, well-balanced life.

Stressed Out? Try These Tips

While we might not be able to change the stress factors in our lives, there is plenty we can do to manage them.

- Keep stressful situations in perspective "Count to 10", and "Don't sweat the small stuff"
- Recognize when you are overwhelmed, and "focus and finish"
- Become a better manager of your time
- Delegate responsibilities and provide clear direction
- Sometimes you need to "just say No"
- Make sure you keep "joy" in your life
- Learn how to recognize and resolve conflict
- Get adequate, restful sleep
- Think of your life holistically and recognize the impact stress may be having on your health and well-being.

13

Designing Your Way: Real Stories

*N*ow that we have identified some key elements to a journey to find a balanced lifestyle, let's put it all together and give you some examples of clients who have made successful transitions from an unhealthy lifestyle that was impacting the quality of their life, to a balanced lifestyle that gave them a better life.

As I've indicated, every journey is different. There is no right or wrong way to get there. It depends on who you are, what you need to address, your likes and dislikes, your knowledge and environment. The important criteria are that you allow yourself to identify and accept your current actions, contemplate how you could change them, and then execute changes as you go – and never give up.

The first journey follows Jill, a single mom who was a yo-yo dieter for years, as she confronts her mental obstacles that have kept her from change, and redirects her attitude and thinking. The second is Dan, a middle-aged HVAC contractor whose weight had gotten so out of control that his life was in jeopardy. His journey is more about education and awareness, and making the decision to actually want to change. Two different paths with the same journey – a better quality of life.

JILL'S WAY

Jill is a single mom, 37, with two children, 12 and 8, who works full time and is trying to advance at her job and be a great mom. She spends her days getting the kids off to school, working and then either shuffling her kids off to practice, attending PTA meetings, or doing errands. Most of the time she feels tired, overwhelmed and sometimes depressed. She never lost her baby weight from her second child, or recovered from her divorce four years ago. She's put on another 20 pounds since, because she is too busy to take care of herself. She does not exercise or eat right, and is an emotional eater. Her weight is making her miserable. She would benefit by losing about 50 pounds, and she worries about developing Type II Diabetes like her overweight mother.

She has tried all the diets – South Beach, Jenny Craig, Nutri-System, you name it; she's been on it. She pretty much wakes up every morning on a diet, only to go to bed with regrets about her failure. She's had some successes with Weight Watchers from time to time. She is successful as long as she goes to her weekly meetings. Inevitably, though, she will gain a few pounds, dread her weekly weigh-in, and before she knows it, she is right back where she started. She has a membership at the gym – $39 taken out of her checking account every month – and she hasn't gone in four months. She feels guilty about that. "I never have time to go!" she justifies. A few years back, when she was still hopeful that her life would get better, she used to dream about being a super mom – in great shape, going to the gym, being the envy of her friends, maybe even dating again? She doesn't even let herself have those types of dreams any more. She simply wallows in her misery as she eats emotionally – the only thing that seems to comfort her is the main thing that is making her miserable.

She considered that maybe her problem wasn't going to be solved by going on another diet. She invested in a few Lifestyle Change Coaching sessions as a last desperate attempt to solve her problem.

After her initial session, she contemplated whether she was ready to take a different path to changing her life. She thought about if she really wanted to be happy. Did she believe she could do this? Could she really become someone who wasn't a slave to diets and could make good decisions on her own? Was she willing to take the time to uncover some of the real problems that were causing her unhealthy lifestyle? While it seemed scary and almost impossible, she decided she was willing to give it a try.

As suggested, she tried to wake up every morning with a positive self-image, look in the mirror and visualize the thinner, happier, more energetic person she once was. And then, pay attention as her day went on – what things got in the way of that energetic person.

She worked on identifying her mental and environmental obstacles that were holding her back. She started observing her actions. What decisions she made and why she made them. What could she have done better? What triggered her behaviors? This is what she discovered:

She recognized she had been in serious denial. She would eat food that she didn't admit to. She would actually sneak food from her children, so they didn't observe her actions and upon further thought, wondered, "Gee, am I sneaking it from myself as well?"

Jill caught herself mindlessly eating several times a day – eating a few chips while making her kids lunch, picking up cookies and other goodies in the coffee room. She would eat fun size Snickers (said she bought them for the kids, but really for herself). Then she would mindlessly eat them – sometimes six or seven a day. And, she allowed herself to believe it was the kids who were eating them, which is funny because her kids don't like nuts!

She was always able to control her food when in front of others but anticipated the joyous time when she could let loose and eat what she wanted when she could be alone. Jill thought she was a fairly healthy eater, but then recognized that while she made attempts to keep her food under control – choosing salads, foregoing the round of desserts at a party, passing up the carbs in the breadbasket – she often gave in to a lot of junk food.

She made excuses and justified her actions nearly every day. Every morning she would vow to take that walk or go the gym at lunch, and she had a myriad of excuses to justify not going. She considered if, maybe sometimes, she deliberately let things get in her way to justify an excuse.

Jill was always stressed out. Going in five different directions trying to please everyone. She realized that food had become her release, her entertainment and sometimes her only friend to comfort her at the end of a long, stressful day. Eating healthy was just one more thing to think about.

Peeling back the layers revealed that dieting contributed a lot to her behaviors. Dieting led her to cheating, which led to guilt, which left her feeling powerless. The various diets she had been on had left her less educated and led to some bad decisions. Chronic stress and her busy life contributed as well. With her negative behaviors identified, she took action to change them.

Jill realized that her excuses for frequent trips to the drive-thru were mistakenly justified by claims of not having enough time or giving in to her kid's requests. The reality is that she barely put up a fight when her kids begged her to go. They always knew it wouldn't take long for Mom to cave in. She realized how long it was taking for her to wait in line. She also opened her eyes to the fact that the foods her kids were eating were really unhealthy. Jill started to eat more foods from home and eventually tried her hand at cooking simple, fast and easy meals. She started buying more produce – only this time she made a commitment to eat them. And, she made it a rule for her kids as well. They complained a lot at first, but since Jill made it her rule too, the kids soon followed. At one point, her daughter said, "Mom, I'm proud of you. I know we complain, but I know you do it just because you love us." Eventually, her daughter got in the habit of starting dinner for Mom on some nights. After a while she realized that eating from home wasn't such a big deal and that the hardest part was giving up the convenient excuses.

Jill also recognized that going to the gym was not going to work for her lifestyle. In accepting this, she allowed herself to let go of her guilt about the $39 monthly charge she'd committed to, and would have to just wait until her contract was up. She started walking – three times around the building during lunch. It was winter, so it was too dark to walk in the evenings. She made a commitment to just move around her house for 20–30 minutes each evening. She would either turn on music or put on Fit TV and follow along with one of the shows. Sometimes her daughter would join her and they would laugh together as they fumbled along. The hardest part for Jill was getting up after sitting down all day. She knew it was always an option to not move, but she remembered that this journey wasn't about weight loss but feeling better both physically and mentally, and she liked how exercise made her feel. That compelling reason gave her the push she needed to put things in motion.

Her mom got her a treadmill for Christmas, and then a lot changed. She was so thrilled; she couldn't wait to use it. Because she was already in the habit of doing her little walks or jumping in front of the TV, she could easily get down to business and burn some serious calories. Jill hated to run so to push herself she used the incline. Sometimes she couldn't believe how far she had come. "I never thought I would actually want to exercise," she admitted.

Giving up her dieting mentality was not easy. She had spent years being a slave to diets and she struggled with making decisions based on what she craved and what her body needed. She accepted that fruits and vegetables would have to be eaten daily, just because it was what her body needed to be healthy, not because it was part of the dieting rule. This shift in thinking made it easier for her to commit to the change, and eventually, if she went without vegetables she just didn't seem satisfied. At times, if vegetables weren't available to her throughout her busy day, she found herself looking in the fridge, with

a craving for something before going to bed and found she effort-
lessly munched on carrots as her decision without sacrifice.

She also had to retrain her education. With all the diet books on
her shelf, she had become confused about what foods she should eat to
lose weight and be healthy. She got educated in the basics and started
to focus on calories and the foods she had been eating. "Have I really
been eating 1000-calorie Caesar salads?" The realization piqued her
interest in what else she was eating. She started surfing the Net, finding nutrition information on her various favorite restaurant foods and
was shocked! She was angry about the revelations, but then she felt
empowered. She dug a little deeper, researching some alternatives
to her favorite foods, and found some substitutes and trade-offs that
could keep her happy and not deprived while minimizing the damage. When she realized that, in moderation, she didn't have to give
up her chocolate she learned to savor and enjoy it instead of sneaking
and denying it. The "in the moment" eating and enjoyment allowed
her to be more satisfied with less consumption.

And, she started eating breakfast, finally admitting to herself that
her old habit of foregoing eating earlier in the day was just a way to
save up, so she could gorge at night with her emotional eating excursions. She still had bouts of emotional eating, but she was able to
control the damage by being aware that she was emotionally eating.
She started to do more thinking about her emotions, rather than eating them.

Jill didn't make these changes overnight, they slowly evolved because she didn't give up. It wasn't as easy as it sounds. She stumbled
a lot, especially in the beginning. Putting her blinders on from time-
to-time, she took a few steps backward but then remembered that
this was par for the course. Rather than beat herself up, she thought
about what made her revert back and learned from the situation. As
she continued on her journey she became more aware of her environment and got more educated, acknowledged her behaviors, and took
action to change them and hold herself accountable. As time went
by, her new habits became easier. While still tempted, she wanted to

maintain control, feel better, and little by little she was able to stay in control.

She learned a lot about herself and how much damage her actions were doing judging not just by the mirror or the scale, but also by how she was feeling physically and emotionally. She had felt so powerless. Coming clean and getting rid of some of her excuses, she realized that denial and blame had been ruling her. She started to really feel good about herself again.

During the journey, there were times of frustration. Jill's weight wasn't coming off as quickly as she had hoped – certainly slower than any diet she had been on. When she felt low this would really bother her, but she knew that this time it was going to be bigger than the scale. She knew that this journey would transform her life, and she was willing to be patient.

Jill's journey continues. She lost 30 pounds in one year and she would still like to drop another 10. The final 10 would be awesome, but for now she likes what she sees in the mirror and she no longer dreads the future. She still has to watch herself from time to time and she sometimes has trouble listening to her body. But she knows that she will never go back to the way she was before. That person is gone, and she has become someone she thought she could never be.

DAN'S WAY

Dan is a 46-year-old HVAC site supervisor who is an ex-football player, married with three kids. Always known and respected as a big, powerful strong guy, he was proud of his big stature and strength. Over the years, the athletic icon had started packing on the pounds. He hadn't weighed himself in a long time, because his scale only went up to 300 pounds.

Over the last few years, Dan had been diagnosed with hypertension and high cholesterol. He also suffered from reoccurring knee pain and sleep apnea. His declining health, medications and increasing size had started to affect his libido and he wasn't feeling so powerful. While he tried to uphold his image, he subconsciously realized that, instead of being a man of great stature, he had become the fat guy. He would go along with the harmless ribbing of his colleagues and friends, acting as if it didn't bother him – but it did.

He loved watching sports, had the cable package subscription and loved to spend time with his buddies. The weekends were all about watching the games along with Buffalo wings, nachos and quite a few beers. He used to play in a softball league and helped coach his son's Little League team, but over the last few years it had become too difficult for him. He sat in his truck a big part of his day, and when home, preferred his recliner and remote control.

A few years back, he tried the Atkins diet. He cut back on carbs and ate nothing but fat and meat. He was successful, dropping 30 pounds. Within months, however, he gravitated back to his old eating habits and gained the weight back – ending up heavier than ever. He didn't even try to exercise. He got out of breath just climbing the stairs.

He had very little education on what foods he should be eating. He ate fast food every day at his job, and ate anything he wanted – not even thinking about nutrition or calories. He was drawn to two-for-one deals and super-sizing for an extra 39 cents. "If it's a bargain – I'm there!" Healthy food was for "wussies" and he reveled in his staunch reluctance to eat anything that was green.

His initial "Ah-ha" moment came when his 14-year-old son made an unintentional sarcastic remark about his declining agility and weight, and he realized that maybe his son was not so proud of him anymore. Around the same time, his employer had implemented a wellness program and, after taking a confidential Personal Lifestyle Profile, he was selected as someone who could benefit from personal assistance and was invited to participate in a Lifestyle Coaching Program. He laughed about it at first, but a little piece of him thought about his son, and maybe he could make him proud of his dad again. He reluctantly agreed to give it a try.

At his first coaching session, he talked about what foods he ate, where he ate them, and what he liked and didn't like. Here was his typical day:

◆ His mornings started early, with a stop at the local gas station for a sausage biscuit, hash browns, a large coffee and a quart of OJ.

◆ Lunch was at the drive-thru. Whatever was the cheesiest, biggest super-sized combo available, along with a jumbo coke.

◆ Dinner started with an after work beer and typically more fat – a pizza his wife brought on her way home from work, mac 'n' cheese, fried chicken or lasagna; trips to the fast food lane after his son's little league game; or beer and appetizers while watching football at a local bar with his buddies.

◆ It looked like he might have a dependency on beer, as he would consume at least a six-pack by the end of the night, and drinking started around noon on weekends.

It was determined that Dan was eating about 4000 calories a day and three times the recommended daily servings of fat and sodium, which of course, contributed to his hypertension and high cholesterol. He rarely ate anything that wasn't mostly fat and sugar. The beer and soda alone contributed to nearly 1000 calories a day. If Dan didn't change his lifestyle, he'd probably be dead within 10 years.

With this information, Dan acknowledged that he wasn't happy with his behavior and did want to do something about it. He was able to take the blinders off and begin to recognize that his actions had huge consequences.

He wasn't so sure what he was going to do with this information. He had to think about it. How was he going to admit to everyone that he was going to change? What if he failed? "Me, a rabbit eating health nut? No way. I'd rather die."

In his next session, he received a few recommendations: Think twice before drinking the last few beers of the night, and either replace the soda with water or try splitting half diet soda with half regular, and see if it was palatable. And, try to slow down while he was eating and think about everything he put in his mouth. He thought that was a weird request but was pleasantly relieved that he didn't have to give up pizza or beer or his other favorites. "This I could do," he thought.

These initial instructions of the coaching were easy for Dan. He did the half diet/half regular soda idea, and was able to nurse his last beer of the evening and not have another. He also bypassed the hash browns in the morning (they weren't very good anyway). He didn't change anything else, but as instructed, he tried to be a little more conscious of his actions and admitted he didn't think he ate as much as he would have.

The first week he didn't lose a pound. He went in complaining. The coach asked him if the changes in his diet were difficult for him. When he said, "No," she said, "Then what's the difference? Maybe you would've gained a pound this week if you didn't make the choices you made?" He decided to forge ahead. They talked about his love for fatty foods, and educated him on calories and the reasons fat can pack on the weight. With this knowledge, he understood that maybe he could cut back a little on some of the fatty and fried foods. He received a list of some resource websites on fast food nutrition values. He was also asked how he felt about starting to be more physically active. He said he would think about it. While he could reminisce about running down the field for a touchdown, he couldn't imagine himself even briskly walking around the block now.

Well, he didn't use the Internet, but he knew his wife was always on Facebook, Ebay and chatting with friends. He thought twice about telling her what he was doing and about the coaching – especially since she used to nag him about his weight from time to time. He didn't want her to get all excited about it – hell, she'd be running out buying tofu hot dogs! He decided to take the risk and ask her about it anyway. To his surprise, she got emotional and cried. He started to listen beyond her nagging and realized that she was really scared about his lifestyle. They talked about how the nagging only made him want to eat more, just out of spite – and if he was going to try this, she was going to have to back off and let him make his own decisions. They agreed.

He asked her to check out the websites the coach was talking about. Careful not to cross any boundaries and without saying a word, she left a list on his desk of some alternatives to his favorite restaurant meals. After trying a few, he seemed to have the best luck with Wendy's, where he could get a large chili and a grilled chicken sandwich for half the calories of the "Baconator" and fries. It worked well, since the chili was more of a comfort food and hit the spot.

He started to drop weight – about two pounds a week – but some weeks he didn't lose any. He was always disappointed with the scale, but he persevered because he wasn't really giving up much and was actually starting to feel a bit better. He wanted to continue in spite of the scale.

One day at work he received a memo, with step pedometers attached, announcing a physical fitness challenge. He distributed it to his men and they joked about it. But then, being competitive, they decided to bet on who could log the most miles. After a few days, the challenge idea petered out, but Dan hung onto his pedometer. He secretly started wearing it, keeping track of his steps every day. Then he started challenging himself. It's not like he took long walks around his neighborhood, but he would simply get out of his truck more, walk around the worksites, or walk the field while watching his son play baseball. As a few more pounds came off, he challenged himself to work on getting to the top of the stairs without being out of breath.

Meanwhile, his wife, who had made a pact with herself to not get overly helpful, started sneaking things in on him. She substituted whole grain pasta for regular, and slowly reduced the amount of cheese and oil she used in cooking. She would bring home thin crust pizza instead of the cheese-stuffed thick crust, and just tell him it was on sale. Sometimes Dan caught on to her efforts, but kept it to himself – he knew she was doing it because she loved and cared about him.

His colleagues and buddies started noticing his change in choices and teased him about it all the time. Dan thought at first that it would bother him, but the teasing was very good-natured and everyone really seemed to be very supportive of him, even proud of him. So, he at least felt better about the teasing shift in focus. He loved to pull at his pants to emphasize how much weight he had lost and brag about it.

As time went on, Dan's choices became easier to make. His appetite wasn't as strong and his "the fattier the better" palate started to change. He still had his wings and beer, but he thought a lot about his actions and often questioned why he was reaching for another beer, another wing or skin. He liked himself better when he was more in control and would sometimes already have his hand on a beer, only to return it to the fridge.

He was still reluctant to eat anything green, but he did start enjoying his wife's homemade stews and soups that had vegetables in them as opposed to fat and cheese. Unfortunately for his wife, it meant fewer stops at the pizza joint and a bit more time in the kitchen, but it was a small price to pay to get her husband healthy again.

Dan stood in front of the mirror one day and, for the first time in a long while, saw a glimpse of that football player in high school. He went into the attic and got out his old weight bench and started lifting. He had been on his journey for about six months and had dropped about 40 pounds. Moving around was becoming a lot easier. He incorporated his weights with some cardio work he remembered from the old days and, while his ability was limited, he forged along. Then, ironically, he got an invitation to his 30th high school reunion. That was all he needed to open the door to unlimited possibilities.

Dan's health statistics were re-measured after one year. His cholesterol levels had fallen to within normal range, his blood pressure was normal, and his libido was – ahem – up. He no longer had sleep apnea symptoms. He has finished his sessions with his Lifestyle Coach, but last I heard, he would be coaching his son's Little League this year.

14

Bon Voyage – Find Your Balance in an Out of Balance World

*D*an and Jill's outcomes were both successful, yet they took different paths to get there and their journey still continues. Your challenge is to find your own individual path to lifestyle change.

A few key points to remember as you coach yourself through this process:

♦ Make sure you are ready to change for the right reasons. While weight loss or achieving health status are important, you have to want to live healthy, not just be healthy. LIVING healthier is in the moment and will help you make the right decisions as you learn to have a balanced lifestyle. You need to not just change what you eat or how you move, but contemplate what has been driving your negative decisions.

♦ Understand that the American lifestyle of today is not normal and is damaging to our health and well-being. Make a decision not to fall victim to it and make the effort to live healthfully in spite of it.

♦ Remove your blinders. Acknowledge what you are doing and be accountable for your actions. Coming clean is a vital step in achieving success. Once you know what has been keeping you from change, you can take steps to fix it.

♦ What you put in your mouth and whether or not you choose to use your body starts in the brain, but the reaction and outcome of those decisions impact the body. With the increasing confusion, information and resistance we experience in today's world, we have been using our brains to make decisions. The typical American lifestyle is most likely influencing your negative thoughts and actions. Changing what drives your decisions is a learning process and takes time, and is easiest to achieve when you practice Accountability, Acknowledgement and Awareness.

♦ By implementing the basic principles of moderation and balance, and getting rid of the mental obstacles that keep you from making good decisions, you can learn how to listen to your body's signals. They will instinctively make the right decision for your good health and well-being, and it can become effortless.

♦ Be patient. Don't expect changes overnight. Lifestyle change is an ongoing journey – it has a beginning but no end. Through gradual changes and adaptation, what you want can change – and it is much easier to implement what you want to do than have to do.

♦ Wipe the slate clean of any confusing dieting logic or manipulation by the food marketing industry, and start following the simple practices of basic nutrition and the realities of weight loss. You may have to invest a little time in getting educated, but once you have the knowledge you need, you can turn off all the other confusing messages and be done with it.

♦ Accept responsibility for taking care of yourself and feed your body first. Provide your body with the nutrition it needs and the activity it craves, and minimize excesses that cause you imbalance.

♦ Physical activity does not have to be timed or structured as defined by "exercise." Any activity is better than no activity. Instead of being resistant to exercise, start by just moving your body more and appreciating how much better you feel for doing it. Recognize that the more mentally resistant you are, the more you probably need it. Getting started is the hardest part. Once you put the activity in motion, the rest is easy.

♦ Consider if stress has been a factor in your inability to lead a better quality of life, and do whatever you can to manage it. Often we get "caught up in it" and we allow it to overtake our lives without recognizing opportunities to control it. When we have chronic stress in our lives, it's easy to forget about the big picture and little things can become overwhelming – we see the glass half empty. Keeping things in perspective and changing your attitude can greatly help your ability to manage stress. Taking care of yourself can give you the best ammunition to achieve this.

♦ Once you identify what is keeping you from change and you get educated on the basic principles of moderation and balance, you can adapt a lifestyle program that fits your lifestyle, your likes and dislikes, and your personal goals. A lifestyle that becomes who you are, not what you are pretending to be.

By slowly adapting to changes and recognizing the positive effects they have on the quality of your life, you can finally become one of "those" people, who seem to eat whatever they want and never gain a pound. One of "those" people who want to exercise, and one of "those" people who seem to be able to manage their lives so well. You will never want to go back to your old lifestyle. It will be forever.

I wish you success in your journey to *Find Your Balance in an Out of Balance World*. Look your best, feel your best and have a happy, healthy life!

Afterword

I mentioned in the book that I encourage you to get educated in the various aspects of your lifestyle change obstacles. There are tons of information available through books and the Internet. The problem is, it can be difficult to know which source to rely upon. The following are some useful, trusted sites you may find helpful:

WEBSITES

www.Mypyramid.gov

Contains lots of great information on personal health and wellness, including calculators that can determine your daily estimated calories and nutritional needs.

http://www.cfsan.fda.gov/~dms/foodlab.html

Provides specific information on how to read a nutrition label, provided by the US Food and Drug Administration. Knowing how to read this label is important, as it will provide you a complete understanding of the value of the foods you are eating.

www.dietfacts.com
www.calorieking.com

Two great sites that provide a comprehensive database on calorie and nutrition values in foods served at chain restaurants and fast food outlets. The menu items are not complete because many restaurants still refuse to provide this information. So, if the menu item is not listed, beware because it is probably one of the worst choices for you.

BOOKS

The Culprit and the Cure by Steven Aldana

By far, this is one of the best books I have read, and it most closely follows the principles I have outlined in this book. It provides a good deal of technical information, but is still an easy-to-understand book of valuable and sensible information.

Breaking Free From Emotional Eating by Geneen Roth

This book goes into detail in the areas of bad habits, emotional eating and other mental obstacles to change.

FINAL NOTE TO EMPLOYERS

As a former Benefits Consultant, I have a particular interest in getting employers motivated to adopt employee health and well-being as part of their corporate culture. I believe this is essential in order to jumpstart our society's return to being a healthier, more productive country. Your employees spend up to one-half or more of their waking hours in the workplace, and the environment you put them in will drive their behaviors. Many of my clients' biggest environmental obstacles are in the workplace, where there is always a donut or other treat staring at them every time they walk into the lunchroom. Many employees sit endlessly at a computer without an activity break, with the odd exception being the unofficial smoking breaks throughout the workday. Chronic stress affects many employees and, while stress can't be avoided, a lot of negative workplace stress can be better managed through good manager training, communication within the organization, and creating a sense that the employer cares about them. Workplace wellness programs can foster employee loyalty within the organization. Investing in your employees' well-being will lower your insurance costs, reduce absenteeism, and improve productivity and morale. It is a win-win situation for everyone. It increases your bottom line and is the right thing to do.

Here are a few websites and other information on Workplace Wellness:

www.WELCOA.org

The most trusted and recommended source for employers who are looking for ideas, resources, trends and data on the design, implementation and maintenance of workplace wellness programs.

www.wellnessproposals.com

This is another great resource site for employers who are looking for information on implementing and maintaining workplace wellness programs.

www.InnovateWellness.com

Innovative Wellness is a results-oriented workplace wellness provider accommodating employers – both large and smal – that is dedicated to ongoing strategic planning to change employees' lifestyle behaviors through innovative solutions.

Healthy Workforce 2010

Part of the Healthy People 2010 Federal 10-year initiative, with the objective of encouraging employers – both large and small – to promote health in the workplace, with a goal of 95 percent participation by the year 2010. Legislation has been proposed that may offer tax incentives to companies who promote wellness in the workplace.